In the many pictures that I have stored in my mind from the burnt-out junes of 40 years, there is none more dramatic and compelling than that of Bradman's small, serenely moving figure in big peaked green cap coming out of the pavilion shadows into the sunshine, with the concentration, ardour and apprehension of surrounding thousands centred upon him and the destiny of a Test match in his hands.

H.S. Altham

BRADMAN REVISITED

The Legacy of
Sir Donald Bradman

A.L. SHILLINGLAW
(co-written by Brian Hale)

**With a Foreword
by Geoffrey Boycott O.B.E.**

**The Parrs Wood Press
MANCHESTER**

First Published 2003

THE PARRS WOOD PRESS
St Wilfrid's Enterprise Centre
Royce Road, Manchester, M15 5BJ
www.parrswoodpress.com

© A.L. Shillinglaw 2003

ISBN: 1 903158 38 9

Printed and bound in Italy

This book is dedicated to my wife Eve, mum, dad and family, together with the many who have encouraged and sustained my love of cricket.

ACKNOWLEDGEMENTS

From an early stage I have enjoyed the collaboration and assistance of my friend Brian Hale. He became an early convert to the cause and as a result became the co-writer of this book.

Special thanks are due to Geoffrey Boycott for his genuine interest in the project and the time given to writing the Foreword.

My gratitude is due to all at The Bradman Museum in Bowral, Australia, in particular Richard Mulvaney and David Wells, for their most helpful support. They have very kindly supplied many of the photographs that appear in this publication.

In different ways invaluable assistance has been received from the following people, to whom I offer sincere appreciation: Howard Hale, David Egurrola, Linda Jones, Peter Booth, Ted Birch, David Crank, Dave Reynolds, John Kennedy, Joan Hale, John Garrett, Dave Clapham, Peter Murray, Sir Alec Bedser, Jack Potter, Philip Derriman, David O'Reilly, Damian Ryan, David Frith, Steve Roper, Professor Adrian Lees, Andy McCormick, Roy Helsdown, David Jones, Malcolm Handley, Alan Jackson, David Leighton, Rt. Rev. David Sheppard and Andy Searle.

CONTENTS

FOREWORD

By Geoffrey Boycott O.B.E.

EVERY CRICKETER AND CRICKET LOVER acknowledges Don Bradman as the greatest batsman ever. We respect his records and wonder at the speed with which he made all those runs. Over the years many contemporary players and writers have given their views about his batting. The Don has even written books expressing his own ideas on his technique and mental thoughts.

This book tries hard to put together almost every view that has been made of his batting - some quite amazing by well-known cricketers. At the time he was considered by many to be unorthodox and not conforming to any text books - a genius who could not be copied - so hardly anyone tried!

So fifty years after the great batsman retired from batting and two years after his death, we are no nearer to understanding what made him so special. We know he had a different stance - an unusual pickup, dancing feet, lightning reflexes and exceptional balance. His certainty of shot plus concentration and mental toughness were second to none. Yet in forty years of playing, watching and commentating on cricket I have seen a number of great batsmen who possessed many of these qualities. Yet all of them were only 50-60% as good as the Don. So was there something else? Or was he just born special? Tony seeks to deal with this question.

My own conclusion is that it was his upbringing more than anything else that shaped his greatness. Trying to hit a golf ball with a cricket stump is a very difficult task for any Test batsman yet as a small boy Bradman did this for hours and hours to amuse himself. That game must have trained and developed his co-ordination of brain, eye and muscle memory to an extraordinary degree. I know from personal experience that if your brain picks up the line and length quickly then it gives you more time to get into position to hit the ball.

Jack Hobbs was the greatest English batsman. His father worked at a college so in his summer holidays young Jack played cricket with the school servants. He used a cricket stump for a bat and had to hit a tennis ball. Jack only played this way for a few weeks of each year yet it was so similar to Bradman's early cricket. Later on Hobbs said: "This simple practise laid a wonderful foundation giving him a keen eye and developing his wrist strokes."

I believe all batsmen are products of their upbringing. Most of us are taught from an early age to "keep the left elbow up" and to "play a straight bat" and to follow the orthodox coaching fundamentals. Bradman had no such coaching or tuition but was self-taught. His childhood game heightened his senses or reflexes and hand-eye co-ordination to exceptional levels so that his judgement was so superior to anyone else. I truly believe that whichever ball sport he had chosen to play, his special grounding would have helped him achieve greatness.

The author of this book tries hard to examine everything about the style and technique which made Don Bradman unique. It is a fascinating and interesting read. If anyone can find the secret of what made him so much better than anyone else then generations of cricketers could become better batsmen.

Based on the development and achievements of Sir Donald Bradman and Sir Jack Hobbs, this book plus my own experiences leads me to believe that we need greater flexibility when introducing youngsters to the art of batting.

Geoffrey Boycott
November 2002
Wakefield, West Yorkshire

PREFACE

DURING THE YEARS SPENT RESEARCHING this book it became clear that Don Bradman's unique success as a batsman was universally held to be due to a combination of factors. These factors, both mental and physical, set him apart from other great players.

By contrast, the batting method by which he achieved his superiority has received barely any attention.

This attitude was underlined for me in June 2001 when I attended a symposium at Lord's, organised by the Menzies Centre for Australian Studies, to commemorate 'The Don' who had passed away earlier in the year.

It was a uniquely enjoyable and memorable occasion attended by many eminent people from the cricket world, including former players and writers.

Significantly, none of the guest speakers in their eulogies gave a mention to Bradman's style of batting, confining their interesting tributes to his many other qualities.

To my thinking, all great batsmen, past and present, must have enjoyed varying combinations of mental and physical strengths. It is difficult to see how they could have attained their status without. I cannot accept that Bradman could be so advantaged in this area that this alone could explain his huge statistical superiority.

But that, it appears, is what we are expected to accept.

In any case, I have found that most of Bradman's supposed advantages - eyesight, for instance - do not stand up to investigation.

This being so, where does it lead us?

Where Bradman was so very different from everyone else was in his style and approach and I came to believe that this was overwhelmingly the biggest factor in his success story.

Technically, from the moment Bradman adopted his closed face, grip and stance, and commenced lifting the bat, it was self-evident the batting mechanism would differ from the orthodox. The purpose of this book, therefore, is to highlight the method which created Bradman's success.

My years of research, including time spent at Liverpool's John Moores University Centre for Sport and Exercise Sciences, have left me with the conviction that the method of batting, evolved by Bradman from a boyhood game using a golf ball and stump, should be accepted and made available for the benefit of future generations of batsmen.

At the moment, as soon as a young aspiring batsman is guided into an orthodox grip and stance, the possibility of such benefits are gone.

I trust the following pages will illustrate the advantages to be gained from Bradman's methods, while highlighting the difficulty of gaining their acceptance from cricket's ruling hierarchy. Inevitably, some sections of this book are therefore of a technical nature.

It is fitting therefore to let The Don speak for himself in this regard when, in the foreword of his own booklet, 'How to Play Cricket', published by the Daily Mail for one shilling in 1935, he wrote:

So then may I ask you to read slowly and at your leisure. Imagine I am chatting to you not in the role of dictator, but in the role of friend, saying quietly: 'Playing in this manner has given me the best results. Have you tried that way? If not it may assist you. Let us talk it over. Perhaps between us your game can be improved.'

After all, is that not the spirit of cricket?

INTRODUCTION

ON THE OCCASION of Sir Donald's 90th birthday the Sydney Morning Herald 'Tribute Edition' published the following extract:

When Ray Martin interviewed the old-time cricketer Bill Brown on television recently, he asked him a question that many wanted to hear answered: What made Don Bradman so much better than everyone else? What really was his secret? As someone who played with Bradman while he was at his peak, Brown was qualified to answer. He spoke of Bradman's speed of movement and the certainty of his batting and told a story or two to illustrate the Don's uncanny ability. Yet somehow the question was left in the air. You felt Brown did not get to the heart of the matter. Of the millions of words written about Bradman over the past 70 years, not many have got to the heart of the matter. The Bradman phenomenon has been analysed from every angle, yet even the people closest to him have found it hard to put their finger on the source of it.

These pages seek to give reason and to justify the following answers to Ray Martin's questions.

Question: What made Don Bradman so much better than everyone else?

BRADMAN REVISITED

Answer: His distinctive `Rotary' method, played from the position of perfect balance, allowed him to be.

Question: What really was his secret?
Answer: Bradman is the best player ever because he was the best co-ordinated player ever.

Background

My interest in cricket began at an early age, and by the time I was ten years old I had developed a fascination for the great game - and its 'folklore'. The second Test Match against Australia was being played in Sydney during the cold dark days of December in 1946, and I'd gone to bed the previous night with England in a promising position.

I rose early next morning to listen to Alan McGilvray's commentary before going off to school. Overnight, Bradman and Barnes were the two 'not out' batsmen and, straining my ears through the static, I was shocked to find they were both still at the wicket. Each went on to make 234 runs.

As a boy I found it hard to believe how any batsman, never mind two, could possibly remain at the wicket long enough to score so many runs without getting out. This was my first real awareness of Don Bradman. In the schoolyard we had convinced ourselves that Hammond and Hutton were just as good and the Don would now be well past his best. How wrong we were!

Being a young boy, I soon put it to one side, and anyway 1947 was the summer of Compton and Edrich when all kinds of domestic records were set which still stand to this day. But my second awakening to Don Bradman was not far away.

In 1948 Australia sent over one of the strongest teams of all time, with fast bowlers Lindwall and Miller proving too hot to handle most of the time. It appeared that all of their batsmen were able to score virtually at will. On one famous occasion the team actually scored 721 runs in a single day against Essex.

However, it was the fourth Test at Headingley which left a lasting impression on my mind. With Australia set 404 runs to win in less than a day, and the worn wicket taking spin, England were firm favourites with Australia given little chance. Don Bradman had different ideas and, as history shows, pulled off one of cricket's great victories. He scored 173 not out and Arthur Morris scored 182.

When cricket resumed after the war Bradman was in his late thirties. Despite indifferent health the runs still flowed - England's bowlers had simply had a six-year respite.

Brought up on Merseyside in wartime Britain my cricket developed naturally, playing with a bat and tennis ball in the street, on concrete, against any wicket we could find. This was how most young lads learned the game. In those days of short supply the lads owning a bat or ball were always the first to be called on to play.

Soon, my own schoolboy cricket was developing, leading to regular selection for Lancashire schoolboys before being chosen to open the batting for the under 15s North of England against the South match, played at Sunderland in 1952. To my disappointment I was stumped after making four runs.

BRADMAN REVISITED

At this time I was unaware that my stance at the wicket was similar to that of Bradman's. It just happened. I felt more comfortable with my bat, closed face, between my feet. However, it was at this stage the seeds of this book were being sown, when, for the first time, a cricket coach took an interest in my play.

"That is not how to bat, you get your left elbow up and place the bat behind the rear foot like this," he told me. No discussion, no reason, no explanation. But I did his bidding. In the coach's eyes, this was the only way to bat.

It was as a batsman that I had gained representative honours at schoolboy cricket; at this stage my bowling had not developed. Subsequently I could never understand why the natural confidence I had when bowling and fielding was absent when batting.

Carrying out this study has provided me with the answer. I had been induced to give up a natural and successful style in order to conform to perceived 'Orthodoxy'.

My career in club cricket was to last for over 40 years in what was then the Liverpool and District Cricket Competition, during the course of which I became a capped Cheshire Minor County player. During this period the introduction of knockout competitions such as the Gillette Cup also enabled me to play against county sides, and therefore Test players. This did not happen often, but high in my memory bank is one such match in 1964 against Surrey at Hoylake, in which I took the wickets of John Edrich and Ken Barrington. We lost the game but the memories linger on. These matches were the closest I came to playing cricket at the very top level, and for this reason, I shall always be grateful for the opportunities these Cup matches provided.

The years playing for my club, Birkenhead Park, were many and fulfilling in so far as the club proved to be one of the most successful, winning a record number of championships. As age started to catch up with me I dropped down to 2nd and 3rd X1 cricket and this entailed a greater interest in helping the younger members of the club. With this in mind, I also re-read Don Bradman's 'The Art of Cricket'.

It was at this time that an umpiring friend of mine, aware of this interest in Bradman, lent me a wonderful little book belonging to his father, entitled 'How to Play Cricket', by Don Bradman, published by the Daily Mail.

A feature of this book is seven separate photographic pullouts of stills depicting stance and backlift through to completion of the main strokes. Typically, Bradman realised the importance of beginners being able to clearly visualise the strokes as he played them in his prime, from beginning to end. I was immediately struck to notice how Bradman appeared to select every stroke and continue its motion from the same advanced position of perfect balance.

A cabinet displaying a photocopy of the pullouts from Bradman's little book was placed outside the Birkenhead Park indoor cricket hall. A note with the pullouts citing the Don's batting record, and drawing attention to the movement of his bat and feet, was pinned up next to it.

BRADMAN REVISITED

Defining Moment

As if by fate, the defining moment leading to the writing of this book took place alongside the 'Bradman Cabinet' when one evening I was discussing the playing of a shot off the back foot with a boy and a very experienced, highly-qualified MCC staff coach. When venturing a contrary view based upon Bradman's style the coach quickly dismissed what I had to say with the comment: "Bradman was unorthodox so is not to be considered."

The closed nature of this instinctive response shocked me, particularly as it was made within feet of the 'Bradman Cabinet'! Driving home that evening I quickly concluded that something was very wrong when the batsmanship of Sir Donald Bradman was being so easily dismissed, without consideration, simply on the grounds of perceived orthodoxy.

My mind went back to the day many years before when, in the same uncompromising fashion, another coach had led me to change, on the spot, a style that had proved successful and was natural to me.

What was this 'orthodoxy' so often slavishly taught while people were persuaded to dismiss, without consideration or question, the play of by far the most successful batsman in cricket history? Who was it who initially established 'orthodoxy'? It is a subject which will be dealt with more fully in later chapters.

A year or so before this incident, while in my mid-fifties I had taken and passed an initial coaching award course from which I believe I learned much. However, I was dissatisfied with some aspects of the course, and

INTRODUCTION

worried that if a seasoned cricketer like myself was uneasy, what would be going on in the minds of beginners?

Subsequently, MCC Staff Coach Dr David Reynolds, one of the two coaches associated with the course, offered me much invaluable assistance by patiently allowing my many growing ideas concerning Bradman to bounce off him.

The difficulty was 'teaching itself'. I knew from many years playing the game that every batsman I had bowled to and every bowler I had faced was 'different', so giving meaning to Bradman's philosophy on coaching which should deal with 'what to do with the ball', not so much 'how to do it'. He also deemed observation and experience to be his main tools in becoming the batsman he was.

It can be said there are basically two types of batsman:

1. Natural - those who learn for themselves.
2. Coached - those who are taught to bat.

When recently the Wisden Cricketers' Almanack announced the chosen five cricketers of the 20th century, it is interesting, and perhaps revealing, that the four batsmen, Don Bradman, Jack Hobbs, Viv Richards and Gary Sobers, were all self-taught natural players. Spin bowler Shane Warne, of course, made up the list.

If every player is different, is it worthwhile trying to teach a similar method to all players? Defensively maybe, but the basic aim of batsmen is to score as many runs as necessary as quickly as possible to win. This belief leads directly to a fundamental aspect in attempting to explain Bradman, because I believe the method Bradman adopted gave him a greater scope to score all around the wicket.

The reason for this view is supported by the following quote of Australian Test batsman Jack Fingleton, in tandem with the words of Bradman himself. Fingleton clearly establishes Bradman's batting style to be fundamentally different to accepted orthodoxy because his bat commenced its motion from a 'closed face between the feet' stance, giving him ideal balance:

Bradman's batting stance is unique. His bat touched the ground between his feet, not behind them like every other batsman and photograph I have seen. He stood perfectly still as the bowler approached, the end of his bat did not act as an escape conductor for energy with that nervous, tap, tap, tap on the pitch so common to most batsmen as the bowler ran to deliver the ball. Bradman at the wicket was completely at ease and at rest until the ball began its apologetic advance towards him.

The implication of this statement will be studied later.

Bradman had this to say when writing about stance in his book 'The Art of Cricket':

I allowed my bat to rest on the ground between my feet simply because it was a comfortable and natural position. It is regarded as more orthodox to

INTRODUCTION

teach a pupil to rest his bat just behind the right toe. This position encourages a straighter backlift, is perhaps sounder for defensive play, but I feel it has greater limitations in versatile strokemaking.

Nothing could be more significant. In Bradman's own words, he suggests that he himself could not have produced the scores he did had he adopted a more orthodox stance which leads to a straighter backlift.

We are dealing with two completely different styles of body motion and batsmanship, commencing from the starting point of grip and stance. Test history indicates that great players, using the more orthodox stance, can attain an average of between 50 and 60 runs, while Bradman, by adopting his 'closed face between the feet' position, recorded an average of 99.94.

It needs to be acknowledged from the outset that, by Bradman's own definition, his style widened the range of scoring possibilities open to him compared to orthodox batsmen. The remarkable versatility and speed of run-getting throughout Bradman's career indicates this to be so.

It is well to remember in any discussions about Bradman that we are talking about a 'superman' only in performance terms. He did not appear to have any of the natural attributes commonly associated with athletes. His general health was at best average, some may say below average. He missed almost a complete season through ill health and Bradman had this to say following a sudden appendix operation near the end of Australia's 1934 tour of England:

BRADMAN REVISITED

There can be no doubt that for some time I hovered on the brink of eternity, which was not nearly so bad for me as for my wife in Australia, who heard the general rumour of my demise. Indeed, you can imagine her anxiety after hearing such news whilst awaiting a phone call to the London hospital. Fortunately, the rumour was exaggerated, by how much, I did not really care.

Even Bradman's eyesight, when tested and compared with students at Adelaide University, was found to be slightly below average. Being about 5 feet 8 inches tall and of slim build, he would be lost in any small groupings of men.

My study commenced from the premise there must be a reasoned explanation for Don Bradman's massive statistical superiority, if for no other reason than the runs were in the book and he put them there. How did he develop and how did he play?

Yet certain questions raised concern and doubt. Why did Bradman not revolutionise batting? After so many years in the spotlight, with scores of books and thousands of articles written about him, why was Bradman still misunderstood?

Nobody has successfully imitated him and the pre-Bradman tenets of technique survive him. He seems to have been generally accepted as a one-off, not just because of his unique style but because of his concentration and temperament. Greg Chappell had this to say: "Bradman was a package of physical and mental talents which apparently have never been found together in another individual." Others simply end the matter by calling him a batting 'genius'.

In batting terms, Bradman was a 'genius' and admittedly the more his scores are digested the more inconceivable they seem. Yet these runs were crafted, however he felt, under all conditions in the days of uncovered wickets, and for those to whom the word 'pressure' has become a phobia, has anybody ever had more placed upon their wicket?

Like the rest of us, whatever the state of the game, Bradman still had to walk out to the middle to face those first uncertain overs, each ball to be treated on its merits and a proper judgement and response made. How was it Bradman so rarely failed, and scored the number of runs he did so quickly?

Because his record was so outstanding, he has been treated as a one-off. There is also a wide variety of opinions amongst his contemporaries about his basic soundness and method which further confuses the issue. This is hard to accept, but most surprising of all, it seems that no fully comprehensive attempt to understand all aspects of his batting has ever been carried out.

Jack Potter, inaugural head coach of the Australian Cricket Academy, confirmed the truth of this to me during three meetings we had about Sir Donald, followed by related correspondence. Being an English club cricketer, it was very generous for an Australian of such standing in cricket to contribute his time exchanging views. This gave me a tremendous boost in confidence when he put his reputation on the line and sent copies of my notes, as he wrote, "to the great man himself". This encouragement, so kindly given, provided much appreciated help whilst fuelling my desire to complete the study.

Other much appreciated and vital assistance came from Professor Adrian Lees, Deputy Director, Research Institute for Sport and Exercise Sciences at Liverpool's John Moores University. Professor Lees was prepared to look at the subject of Don Bradman's batting with an open mind and we were able to conduct a series of tests using video recordings from six different angles on batsmen employing both the orthodox and Bradman methods of striking a cricket ball.

High-speed motion analysis was used to investigate whether the Bradman technique for batting could be considered at least equal to the orthodox technique when fulfilling the basic principals of batsmanship. The conclusion was: the Bradman technique appears to have no disadvantages compared to the orthodox technique in terms of time to complete a stroke, and the speed of the bat at impact. My own belief, supported by Bradman's own words, is that his method goes beyond parity and offers greater scope and possibilities in scoring runs which I feel sure will be established scientifically at a future date.

Professor Lees kindly produced a written preliminary report of his findings, a copy of which was sent to the MCC technical department at Lord's. A copy of this report was also submitted to the Liverpool Daily Post, and when an article by Malcolm Handley appeared in the 25th April 2000 edition, it sparked a remarkable reaction.

INTRODUCTION

Next morning most national daily newspapers carried their own comments including, amongst others, reports in The Times, Daily Telegraph and Daily Mail. Within two days of these reports in England, Australia's Sydney Morning Herald had responded with comments of its own.

Before the day was out, Professor Lees and myself had been interviewed on both English and Australian radio, and within ten days news reports had been shown on both Sky TV and Australian Channel 9 TV.

What this remarkable response proved is that cricketers the world over are as keen as ever to understand how and why Bradman achieved such superiority.

The realisation that nobody has an understanding of Bradman's batting suggests a clear opportunity to approach the subject of his batsmanship with an open mind, if for no other reason than the outstanding record of his success demands it.

The following chapters seek to outline not only something of the man, his record, how others view him and the influence he still holds on the game, but more importantly they seek to give reason and explanation to the source and developing process which I believe lead to the unique batting motion of Don Bradman.

The intention of this book is for the methods of both Bradman's development and technique to be understood and accepted for the benefit of future generations of batsmen.

PART ONE

Setting the Scene

1.

COMPARING FIGURES

This book is not another detailed analysis of Bradman statistics. It is not of course possible to write a book about him without drawing attention to his unique achievements with the bat - and I use the word unique in its literal sense. Statistics are therefore brief and their purpose is to set the scene and justify the years of research which have gone into the production of this book. I am concerned to show that behind the genius that was Bradman lay a style which stands up to any criteria of judgement and which can be used to advantage by any budding batsman with the determination to succeed. They may not emulate the Don's amazing feats, but if they can become better players - who can say?

The following table shows a statistical comparison between some of the best known batsmen from each of the major test-playing countries using a minimum of 2500 runs as a qualification.

Great Batsmen Comparisons

	M	Inns	NO	Runs	HS	100s	Ave	%100s
D. G. Bradman (A)	52	80	10	6996	334	29	99.94	36.25
R. G. Pollock (SA)**	23	41	4	2256	274	7	60.97	17.07
G. A. Headley (WI)**	22	40	4	2190	*270	10	60.83	25.00
H. Sutcliffe (E)	54	84	9	4555	194	16	60.73	19.04
E. Paynter (E)**	20	31	5	1540	243	4	59.23	12.90
K. F. Barrington (E)	82	131	15	6806	256	20	58.67	15.26

SETTING THE SCENE

Name							
E. D. Weekes (WI)	48	81	5	4455	207	15	58.61	18.52
W. R. Hammond (E)	85	140	16	7249	*336	22	58.45	15.71
G. S. Sobers (WI)	93	160	21	8032	*365	26	57.78	16.25
S. R. Tendulkar (I)	105	169	16	8811	217	29	57.58	17.16
J. B. Hobbs (E)	61	102	7	5410	211	15	56.94	14.70
C. L. Walcott (WI)	44	74	7	3798	220	15	56.68	20.27
L. Hutton (E)	79	138	15	6971	364	19	56.67	13.77
G. S. Chappell (A)	87	151	19	7110	247	24	53.86	15.89
A. D. Nourse (SA)	34	62	7	2960	231	9	53.81	14.51
Inzamam-ul-Haq (P)	85	140	13	6214	329	17	53.57	12.14
R. Dravid (I)	69	118	13	5614	217	14	53.46	11.86
Javed Miandad (P)	124	189	21	8832	*280	23	52.57	12.16
S. M. Gavaskar (I)	125	214	16	10122	*236	34	51.12	15.88
A. R. Border (A)	156	265	44	11174	205	27	50.56	10.18
I.V.A. Richards (WI)	121	182	12	8540	291	24	50.23	13.19
D.C.S. Compton (E)	78	131	15	5807	278	17	50.06	12.98
S. R. Waugh (A)	156	245	42	10039	200	22	49.45	10.19
B. Mitchell (SA)	42	80	9	3471	189	8	48.88	10.00
G. Boycott (E)	108	193	23	8114	*246	22	47.72	11.40
E. J. Barlow (SA)	30	57	2	2516	201	6	45.74	10.52
Saeed Anwar (P)	55	91	2	4052	*188	11	45.52	12.09
M. D. Crowe (NZ)	77	131	11	5444	299	17	45.36	12.97
G. M. Turner (NZ)	41	73	6	2991	259	7	44.64	9.58
A. Flower (Z)	63	112	19	4794	*232	12	44.40	9.09
A. H. Jones (NZ)	39	74	8	2922	186	7	44.27	9.45
P. A. De Silva (SL)	93	159	11	6361	267	20	42.97	12.58
S. T. Jayasuriya (SL)	76	128	12	4789	340	10	41.28	7.81

* Indicates Not Out

** Included for their outstanding figures

N.B. Figures of current Test players up to March 1st 2003

17

2.

THE YOUNG BRADMAN

An Enigma

Having established just how uniquely good a batsman Bradman was and shown his style to be different from 'accepted orthodoxy', it is essential to begin to understand the development which led to Bradman's mastery of his batting skills.

It has been pointed out that Bradman was a 'superman' only in performance terms and very significant to the reasoning behind this study was the fact that when the professor of physics at Adelaide University tested Bradman's eyesight, he discovered Bradman's reaction to be minutely slower than that of the average university student.

Quite naturally most of what has been written about Bradman centres upon his remarkable first class and Test Match career commencing when, as a 19 year old debutante, he took two fours from the first over when he faced great Australian slow bowler Clarrie Grimmett on the way to scoring 118 runs for New South Wales v South Australia, coincidentally at the Adelaide Oval in December 1927.

Exhaustive material has described every conceivable aspect of every first class innings Bradman played and the runs he scored; yet strangely nobody has imitated him. We know everything Bradman did, yet do not know what enabled him to do it.

Perhaps this is because too much emphasis has been given to his first class record to the exclusion of his development. To score a century first up against such as Clarrie Grimmett is unusual in itself, but how did he come to possess the necessary skill and certainty to play such an innings when so young and inexperienced? By all accounts, Bradman was completely self-taught and had played hardly any structured cricket at all up to the age of 17 years.

When beginning this attempt to explain Don Bradman's batsmanship, it soon became apparent that careful study of his own written work was the way to start. By good fortune, when Bradman finished playing he felt it was perhaps his duty to put on paper his theories about how the game should be played, and so applied his lucid cricketing brain and knowledge to writing 'The Art of Cricket'.

Mention has already been made of the short instructional book Bradman wrote in 1934, 'How to Play Cricket'. The film taken to demonstrate the strokes shown in this book was taken when Bradman was batting in his prime. Fortunately, with the advance of technology this film has been adapted to produce an instructional video in which Bradman himself talks us through the strokes as he played them. There is little need to look elsewhere to study his method and technique. Just as Bradman had written about his theories in 'The Art of Cricket', on retirement he also reflected his whole cricketing life through another book, 'Farewell to Cricket'. Bradman wrote and spoke about cricket in the same manner as he played - simply and without complication.

In 'Farewell to Cricket', the significance of the opening chapter, 'In the Beginning', highlights the approach I have chosen to explain the batsmanship of Don Bradman. The following pages set out Bradman's own account of how he developed the amazing skills and performances which led to him scoring the first of his 117 centuries in only 338 first class innings.

Bradman's Beginnings

Bradman's first cricket match occurred when he was 11 years of age, at Glebe Park, Bowral; not a cricket ground but on the football pitch. The pitch was plain dirt and was the most level piece of earth available. Arriving at the crease on a hat-trick, Bradman carried his bat for 55 runs.

When at 'high' school Bradman only played two matches. In the first, at the age of 12 years, he played against Mittagong on a concrete pitch covered in coir matting and out of his team's total of 156 runs Bradman contributed 115 not out; his first century. In the second match, Bradman scored 72 not out. So in competitive matches at school, he scored 242 runs without losing his wicket.

Aged 13 years, Bradman played his first game of senior cricket. His uncle was captain of Bowral and the young Bradman was to be the scorer in a match at Moss Vale when a player failed to turn up. Taking the player's place at the fall of the eighth wicket, Bradman, still in short trousers and holding a man's full size bat, was 37 not out when the last wicket fell. The following Saturday when the match was continued, Bradman was allowed to open the second innings and this time was 29 not out at stumps.

Leaving school at the age of 14 years, Bradman had only batted five times, yet had not been dismissed while scoring 308 runs. When 15 years old he devoted the whole summer to tennis and did the same the following year until playing three games of cricket for Bowral towards the close of the season. Bradman failed to trouble the scorer, out first ball in the first innings, doing little better in the second. However, in a semi-final against Wingello he contributed a top score of 66 for his side.

With the beginning of the summer of 1925, Bradman really commenced his serious cricket career as a regular member of the Bowral team as a 17 year old. Some of his colleagues were in their forties and he deemed it quite a privilege to have the opportunity to play with these grown men.

At this stage I would like older readers to draw upon their own experience by casting their minds back to their developing years and subsequent entry into senior play. It is fair to say that for most of us, the biggest single leap we make in the game is from schoolboy to the tough adult world of cricket. Younger readers may wish to exercise their imagination and assess their ambitions when reaching 17 years of age.

During his first season of adult cricket, and at this age with only eight innings behind him, Bradman made 1318 runs at an average of 101.30 including a District record score of 300, and another score of 234 made against an emerging Bill O'Reilly - who was to become one of Australia's greatest bowlers. According to Bradman himself, the greatest. O'Reilly was to comment: "I could not assimilate the knowledge that a pocket-sized schoolboy could give me such a complete lacing."

Putting such a run-scoring performance into perspective is not easy, but I played 1st X1 club cricket with Birkenhead Park in the Liverpool and District Cricket competition for many post-war years, and during the 50 year span between 1949 and 1999 the batting record for a season was held by Dr John Winter of Northern CC, who, in 1955, scored 1423 runs at an average of 88.93, including eight centuries. John Winter's record was a single peak covering many top batsmen over a 50-year period and was achieved when greatly experienced and batting at the height of his maturity.

So the question is what led a 17 year old, who up until then, was the scorer of only 375 runs in his life, into having the capacity to immediately reach such a peak and go on to produce the phenomenal batting record the cricketing world is now familiar with without ever having a significant lapse in form at any level he played?

The following is Bradman's full account of his cricket and sporting experience up until the time of that first match played at Glebe Park, Bowral, when he carried his bat for 55 runs as an 11 year old, when it soon became clear that much of his instinct and style had already been assimilated:

My education commenced in the normal way. I attended the Bowral Intermediate High School, and although our educational facilities were much the

*same as those at any other school, there was little
or no organised sport for the children in the
primary school.*

*Our headmaster, Mr A. J. Lee, was a good sport
who often amused himself by playing with the boys,
but there was no coach. We were left to our own
devices and had to play as nature advised, without
knowing whether we were adopting orthodox
methods or not.*

*During weekends and after school, I usually
found myself without any playmates because no boy
lived close to our home. For this reason I had to
improvise my own amusement, and this, during the
hours of daylight, almost invariably centred around
the use of a ball. It was either kicking a football,
playing tennis against a garage door or an unusual
form of cricket which I invented for my own
enjoyment.*

*At the back of our home was an 800-gallon water
tank set on a round brick stand. From the tank to the
laundry door was a distance of about eight feet. The
area under-foot was cemented and, with all doors
shut, this portion was enclosed on three sides and
roofed over so that I could play there on wet days.
Armed with a small cricket stump (which I used as a
bat) I would throw a golf ball at this brick stand and
try to hit the ball on the rebound. The golf ball came
back at great speed and to hit it at all with the round
stump was no easy task.*

*To make my game interesting I would organise
two sides consisting of well known international*

names and would bat for *Taylor, Gregory, Collins* and so on in turn.

The door behind me was the wicket, and I devised a system of ways to get caught out, and of boundaries. Many a time I incurred mother's displeasure because I just had to finish some important Test Match at the very moment she wanted me for a meal.

The open side of my playing area corresponded to the on side of a cricket field, and therefore I did not have to chase the ball for any shots on the offside.

This extraordinary and primitive idea was purely a matter of amusement, but looking back over the years I can understand how it must have developed the co-ordination of brain, eye and muscle which was to serve me so well in important matches later on.

Another form of amusement was to take a golf ball into the neighbouring paddock where I would stand some 10 or 15 yards from the dividing fence and throw the ball to hit the rounded rail. My main purpose was to make the ball come back at various heights and angles so that I could catch it. Obviously this also developed the ability to throw accurately, because if I missed the selected spot, it would mean a walk to retrieve the ball.

The playground of the primary school was separated from that of the high school by a fence, but we had the privilege of standing at the gateway. I was frequently to be found at that gateway *watching the senior boys play cricket, and once or twice at their invitation managed to have a few hits with them.*

Even in the senior school playground, there was no cricket pitch and our practice was carried out on dirt, which resembled Nottingham marl in appearance. Our wicket was the bell post. A chalk mark indicated the height of the stumps, and many an argument ensued as to whether the post had been struck above or below the chalk mark.

Bats mainly consisted of pieces of wood from a gum tree, fashioned after the shape of a baseball bat. Pads were never worn, and the ball was of a type commonly known as a 'compo'. A boy usually occupied the crease until he got out.

It seems that during all of Bradman's juvenile development he applied his own initiative and used primitive cricket equipment under difficult conditions while adopting his own style of untutored play. This, I believe, created the Bradman style that remained largely intact throughout his cricketing life.

"The golf ball came back at great speed and to hit it at all with a round stump was no easy matter." A typical Bradman understatement of course, but it is important to appreciate that he was simply amusing himself. His sole aim would be to control the fast moving golf ball as it bounced first from the brick wall and then the cement floor. Little did Bradman realise he was learning to conform to Walter Hammond's idea: "A good shot is one that controls the ball."

BRADMAN REVISITED

Bradman was not learning to bat in a technical sense but was developing, to a highly-tuned degree, all the human senses necessary to become a top class batsman. It is important to point out that there is a sequence of judgements and movements which take place prior to, and during, the actual playing of strokes, each being dependent on the other in order to achieve good timing.

1. Watch the ball and concentrate.
2. Assess line, length, speed and flight of the ball.
3. Select stroke to be played.
4. Pick up and develop the motion of the bat with co-ordinated body movement and footwork towards the point of playing the ball.
5. The quality of the stroke played flows directly from the judgement and motion of the preceding four phases.

It is no use knowing how to play strokes without being in the correct position at the right time to play them. Taking the above points in sequence, the first requirement is to concentrate and watch the ball.

The acute difficulty of the exercise Bradman was performing clearly demanded maximum focus, the value of which is highlighted when he states: "The two most important pieces of advice I pass on to young batsmen are to (a) concentrate and (b) watch the ball."

They could well be the last words before anyone goes in to bat. On this subject Bradman wrote:

SETTING THE SCENE

Concentration can and must be cultivated by anyone who wishes to rise to international standards. It is one of the essentials.

This view is endorsed by C. B. Fry, who was an outstanding and influential English cricket captain and theorist when he made the following penetrating comments on concentration:

There is probably a greater difference between good batsmen in the simple matter of how much they look at the ball than in what amount of manual skill they possess. But the power of watching the ball completely is not in the majority of players a natural faculty; it needs to be cultivated and made an unconscious and subconscious habit; while the visual concentration remains a conscious effort, it is not only liable to break down but is very tiring.

It is important to note that both Bradman and Fry stress the need to 'cultivate' concentration. Bradman's early training made concentration an instinctive habit.

This, of course, is exactly what Bradman did and explains the remarkable concentration and relative lack of tiredness, which enabled him to play so many long innings. Equally, lack of the qualities set out by Fry explains why apparently 'set' batsmen often make mistakes of judgement and get out.

The second and third requirement of controlling the golf ball would be to assess instantly its line, length, speed and flight in order to select the stroke to be played.

From this information the brain would decide the best position to get into in order to hit the fast-moving ball. In batting terms, the linking of these two processes can be classified as 'judgement', the importance of which was brought home to me when I read Bradman's three-word answer to the following question that was put to him. He was asked why he thought a certain player of immense potential had failed to realise that potential. "He lacked judgement" was Bradman's reply.

The fourth requirement is to get into the ideal position at the right time to control the hit and requires quick instinctive footwork, the necessity of which is again expressed first by Bradman and secondly by C. B. Fry as follows:

Bradman:

I doubt if one could truthfully say there is a single key to batsmanship, but footwork is certainly one of the keys to unlock the innermost secrets. It is to batting what a foundation is to a house. Without it there can be no structure.

C B Fry:

It may seem absurd to say that what he does or leaves undone with his feet makes much more difference to a batsman than what he does or leaves undone with his hands, for it is by means of his footwork, and this means alone, that he can bring his bat into effective relation with the ball. It is only by appropriate movement of one foot or the other - or of first one then the other - that the various well-known strokes are possible.

SETTING THE SCENE

It matters how you move your feet after the ball has left the face of the bat as well as how you move them before. For with the feet rigidly fixed, not only is it impossible to begin the stroke correctly, but it is impossible to finish the stroke freely. The fixity of the feet pins the shoulders, and thus reduces the power of following through to practically nil.

Having assumed a position to hit the ball, few would disagree with Bradman's words: "To hit it at all with a round stump was no easy matter."

Yet once in position, Bradman found how best to hit and control the erratically moving ball. He goes on to say:

This rather extraordinary and primitive idea was purely a matter of amusement, but looking back over the years I can understand how it must have developed the co-ordination of brain, eye and muscle which was to serve me so well in important matches later on.

Because of the extreme difficulty of the exercise he was able to perform, it is likely that Bradman instinctively developed the human senses necessary for batting to a degree greater than any player before or since. During this stage, technique would not have been a consideration; the sole focus would be control of the bouncing ball.

More importantly, Bradman was co-ordinating his control of the cricket stump (later his bat) with brain, eye and muscle as an integral part of an instinctive batting motion. He described it thus: "The sight of the ball seems to trigger off a corresponding reaction so that movement becomes almost a habit."

There are many who look upon Bradman simply as a genius who was born to score runs; this attitude being one of the main reasons his batting has remained misunderstood for so long. Certainly he possessed a great natural talent but it is hard to believe that this talent was so much greater than any other player in Test Match history, which points towards Bradman's individualistic early training and subsequent unique batting style as being the main reasons allowing for his success.

When writing about the need to cultivate the essential batting requirements of concentration and watching the ball, Bradman had this to say:

Blessed is the boy who finds himself possessed of these attributes as a natural gift. But like the boy prodigy who, at say the age of five, finds himself able to play the piano, practice and more practice is needed to perfect his talent.

I would counsel every boy who is interested in batting, to play with a ball at every opportunity. Whether it be a golf ball, baseball or any other kind, it doesn't matter. It will help train the eye and co-ordinate the brain, eye and muscle. The early formative years of a boy's career can have a tremendous bearing on his technique.

These words highlight the importance he places in hard practice. Not for him the excuse of such words as 'genius' to describe his success. In 'The Art of Cricket', he simply says: "I don't care who the player is or how great his skill, there is no substitute for proper practice."

Don Bradman was brought up to a healthy outdoor life and, like many other boys, this centred on playing with a ball. Circumstances meant he often had nobody else to play with so quite naturally, he devised his own game, little realising at the time the extraordinary skills he was developing.

Much has been written about Don Bradman since his passing and, considering his achievements, what has shone through and caused so much admiration has been his sincere matter of fact modesty and simple belief that he was a normal human being. By way of explanation, nothing is more natural for a boy than to play, and, in Bradman's eyes, this was all he was doing in that eight foot space beside his home; and he never claimed otherwise.

The Importance of Golf Ball and Stump

Most of the writings on Don Bradman have been happy to explain him away in the simplest terms. His success has been put down to a combination of character, determination, extra sharp reflexes, keen eyesight and perhaps a few other things, both mental and physical. The technique he used to control his shots has received little attention. Indeed, when his technique was mentioned it was usually in a derogatory manner. Aesthetically, his style did not please the purists, and to some, even worse, it was seen as an offence.

Before considering the technique he used in competitive cricket, it is necessary to return to the beginning. What happened during those formative years when, as a boy, he first developed a passion for the game?

In this regard it is impossible to exaggerate the importance to him of the little game he played with golf ball and stump, as described previously in this chapter. I would ask the reader to contemplate the difficulty of controlling a golf ball under the conditions he set for himself. Even better, those interested should try it for themselves.

A golf ball bouncing from brick wall to concrete floor then to be met with the stump requires total concentration. Eye and brain together have to instantly assess speed, flight, line and length in order for the physical co-ordination to take place in time to control the ball in the required manner.

This exercise achieves, to a high degree, the batting requirements of concentration, watching the ball, shot selection and correct footwork. It is well to remind ourselves that Bradman considered the first two of these as of "greater importance than all the theories".

The extreme focus required to hit a ball under these circumstances and the constant practice required to obtain continuation of the exercise brings home the difference between normal concentration and concentration as applied by Bradman. This became clear during my own experimentations but was confirmed to me by coach Dr

SETTING THE SCENE

Dave Reynolds who experienced it for himself during a demonstration at the end of one of his coaching sessions. So impressed was Dr Reynolds, that he took time out to telephone me his interesting little story which was as follows.

As Don Bradman had recently passed away, he had been the subject of some discussion. A fellow coach had suggested to Dr Reynolds that for the final exercise they should use a cricket stump and tennis ball. Being over 50 and wearing spectacles, Dr Reynolds was more than a little aware he could make himself look ridiculous, but nonetheless took up the challenge. He found the result remarkable. After a lifetime in cricket as a wicket-keeper, the degree of watchfulness and concentration required was on a different level to anything he had experienced before. He found he could actually focus on the 'hairs' of the tennis ball as he played it.

This indicates how Bradman developed his twin first principles of 'concentration and watching the ball', while understanding how the exercise demands getting into line and as close to the ball as possible.

In his game therefore, Bradman accomplished all the requirements of a batsman getting into position to control a ball. The fact that he had to do this at such a pace sharpened his thinking processes enabling his later famed aggressive intent to flourish naturally in a balanced, flexible manner, and with a solid foundation. In this way, whilst amusing himself, he unwittingly found the best way for him to control the stump and, therefore, the ball. He had no time to consider how he did so - it was an irrelevance; simply sufficient that he did.

BRADMAN REVISITED

Bradman's chapter 'In the Beginning', previously referred to, draws attention to immediate and exceptional success in his first introduction to cricket as an 11 and 12 year old, right through to his record-breaking first season playing for Bowral. He simply carried this on throughout his first class and Test Match career. My belief is that his greatness is best explained by his training with golf ball and stump. His style was largely set even before he took his first knock in the middle.

During the early days of this study, when wrestling with the problems involved, I was reminded by my wife, Eve, of a well-known saying: "In character, in manner, in style, in all these things, the supreme excellence is simplicity."

It seems very appropriate as Bradman's volume of runs and sheer consistency meant his method had to be simple to him. The bowlers of the world soon found out that given the control he had taught himself over a fast moving ball, he was then quickly able to master the basics of stroke play and batsmanship. It could be said that Bradman is the best player ever, because he was the best co-ordinated player ever.

As he left boyhood behind and joined the man's world of adult cricket, he had already established his style, although his technique had not yet come under proper scrutiny. His 'back yard' game had so honed his cricketing sense that in his few school games he had been virtually invincible. His grip and stance were balanced and comfortable, and crucially his concentration and method had become, in Fry's words, "a subconscious and unconscious habit". The hours of practice on his own proved he had not only the interest but also the determination to succeed.

3.

THE DON ARRIVES

Setting the Standard

Don Bradman had his introduction to State cricket for New South Wales in 1927/28 at the age of 19 years. In less than a full season, batting at six or seven in the order, he finished with an average of 46.22. It was a good start for a youngster, but not exceptional. In a twenty-year career, it would be the only time a Bradman season could be so characterised.

The following season, 1928/29, he scored a record number of runs, 1690 in twenty-four innings, and his top score of 340 was a record for the Sydney cricket ground. England were touring and he made two Test centuries, finishing with the outstanding average of 66.85. At the age of 20 the cricketing world began to pay serious attention.

Twenty years later, playing his final full season in Sheffield Shield cricket, he scored a record eight centuries and averaged 129.60. For the whole of this time his style had remained unaltered. He did not feel it necessary to make any adjustments to accommodate batting at the very top level. What he had developed as a boy, he kept. He was later to write:

SETTING THE SCENE

One thing in particular caused me a lot of thought. I noticed that my grip, developed on concrete wickets, was different from that of most players. It assisted me in pulling a ball and was much safer for on-side shots - though it handicapped me sometimes playing the ball between mid-off and point. I experimented, worked out the pros and cons and eventually decided not to change my natural grip.

Throughout a long career my grip caused many arguments but I think it sufficient to prove that any young player should be allowed to develop his own natural style providing he is not revealing an obvious error. A player is not necessarily wrong because he is different. The use of the wrist and arms and the method of stroke production cannot be stereotyped.

Mention has already been made of how Jack Fingleton, who partnered Bradman in many a big stand, was intrigued by his 'different' stance at the wicket. It is clear that Bradman was seen to be different even before he made a move. To this can be added his demeanour - he was noted for walking out to the wicket and taking guard with a half-smile on his face!

It is apparent that Bradman's self-taught batsmanship caused bewilderment and consternation to those versed in 'orthodoxy'. This was particularly true of English 'experts', who first came across him during Percy Chapman's tour in 1928/29 - but was by no means confined to the English. From the outset, however, Bradman was possessed of a complete confidence and certainty in his own distinctive method.

During the 20th century, a number of great batsmen would fleetingly reach for the heights maintained by Bradman over his twenty-year period, so what allowed him alone the ability to sustain it? Australian cricket writer R. S. Wittington once wrote:

> Bradman's batting convinces me that if his body was only hanging together by strips of adhesive tape he would still score a century.

Cricket Folklore and the Development of Style

Before we can begin to tackle the question posed in the previous chapter, it is necessary to look briefly to cricket's origins in England.

In the early 19th century bowling was underarm and batsmen developed a natural side-on stance, using a straight sideways movement of the shoulders and bat 'to defend their wickets'. So began the evolution of batsmanship.

In 1835 round-arm bowling was allowed, to be followed by over-arm bowling, as we know it, in 1864. It was roughly at this time, towards the late 1800s, that cricket became fashionable under the huge influence of the game's first superstar, W.G. Grace. It was W.G. who was largely responsible for the development of all-round batsmanship off front and back foot.

SETTING THE SCENE

(Interestingly, the few old newsreels of Grace which exist, show his initial bat movement was out towards gully!).

During the later Victorian and Edwardian eras, subsequently to be called by many 20th century cricket writers 'the golden age', perceived style became the order of the day, and it was natural for batsmanship to reflect these attitudes. This was particularly true in England where 'gentlemen' were invariably batsmen rather than bowlers. Indeed, the bowlers at practice were considered to be participating merely for the benefit of the batsmen. Cricket was overwhelmingly dominated by the middle classes, and a look through the record books of pre-World War One clubs shows that the professional classes, such as solicitors, doctors, accountants and schoolmasters, predominated. Overwhelmingly, they were the product of the English public school system, which is where they learned to play cricket. In the scorebooks they were referred to as 'Mr', with their full initials. This lasted until well after the Second World War.

There were many outstanding figures in this so called 'golden age', some of the best known being Ranjitsinhji, C. B. Fry and Gilbert Jessop in England; Victor Trumper, Clem Hill and S. E. Gregory in Australia. C. B. Fry has already been quoted in earlier chapters and it is perhaps worth a more detailed look at this remarkable man. Bill Frindall, the well-known cricket statistician, set the scene when he wrote:

Charles Fry was an exceptionally talented all round athlete and a brilliant scholar and conver-

sationalist, who in modern times would have more than matched the combined attributes of Daley Thompson and Mike Brearley. After captaining Repton (his public school) he gained 'blues' at cricket, soccer and athletics, only narrowly missing a fourth at rugby because of injury. As a fleet-footed full-back he played soccer for England against Ireland in 1901, and for Southampton in the 1902 FA Cup Final. In addition to being an outstanding sprinter, he shared the world long jump record of 23 feet 5 inches for 21 years. He gained first class honours in Classical Moderation. Beyond all those varied triumphs he is best remembered for his batting performance. His technique was based on determination, concentration and a flawless defence; it was evolved from detailed analysis of the game's mechanics. A ferocious straight driver, he favoured the back foot and was particularly strong on the leg side.

His other commitments restricted his appearances abroad and he declined two tours of Australia. He led Sussex for five seasons and was England's undefeated captain during the 1912 Triangular Tournament. He edited his own monthly magazine, wrote a definitive analysis of batsmanship and several other books including an autobiography, and reported and broadcast cricket until his death. He represented India at the League of Nations and was offered - and declined - the throne of Albania.

SETTING THE SCENE

It is difficult to imagine a man with so much and so varied a talent. It is enough to take the breath away and makes it easy to understand how such a person became a major cricketing influence in the 20th century. He wrote his penetrating analysis of batsmanship at the turn of the century and it is likely to be the basis of today's coaching. His explanations regarding footwork, bat movement and concentration are profound and have proved a source of inspiration in the writing of this book. It is possible that modern technology will confirm some of his expositions, in which case it may well also require a re-think on some aspects of modern coaching. What Fry so eloquently wrote about, Don Bradman unwittingly and instinctively put into practice as a boy at play with his golf ball and stump.

Fry and his contemporaries grew to prominence in an era when basic batting principles had already become established in the public schools and universities. The first of these principles is that if the bat is taken straight back, it is more likely to come straight down. To 'play with a straight bat' became part of the English vernacular and had straightforward, upright, honest - and defensive - connotations. Fortunately for this era, formalised coaching was in its infancy and did not stifle the talents of the less orthodox players such as Ranjitsinhji and Gilbert Jessop. Jessop, nicknamed 'the croucher' because of his unusual stance, scored his runs throughout a long career at a rate that dwarfed anyone else - including Don Bradman, but then he was an all-rounder and his batting average of 32 was modest.

BRADMAN REVISITED

Ranjitsinhji was a cricketing icon. He played little cricket as a boy and was only recognised at Cambridge University as talented and awarded his 'blue' during his final year. Most writers in England listed him as one of the all-time greats and hailed him as bringing a new dimension to batting. He was totally unorthodox and recognised as such at the time.

So two of England's greatest 'golden age' cricketers were acknowledged to be different and unorthodox. It is clear that even in Edwardian England there was an accepted orthodoxy. Cricket had assumed the 'pendulum straight bat' as the proper basis of stroke play and to this day the MCC Masterclass video advocates this method of teaching young players. This point will be dealt with more fully later in the book.

In his autobiography 'A Life Worth Living', C. B. Fry had this to say concerning the three Australians I have named from cricket's 'Golden Age':

Victor Trumper used to walk to the wicket and start making beautiful strokes from his first ball onwards. No matter how good the bowling he made it look easy and he never permitted any wicket to appear difficult. He had a natural grace of movement and played his strokes with a swing from the wrists which was not a flick but rather, as it were, a stroking effect.

If Trumper was a stylist for charm, S. E. Gregory was a stylist for correct technique. No man who has ever played cricket could have more usefully been offered to a young cricketer as an example for the standard strokes.

SETTING THE SCENE

Finally, in a reference to Clem Hill, Fry wrote that most critics would select him as "the best left-handed batsman there has ever been", and, comparing him to another great Australian from the same era, Joe Darling, Fry wrote that Hill was the more accomplished on "technical grounds". Given that Fry wrote his book in 1939, this was still exceptional praise for an outstanding batsman.

What is obvious from these brief references to the 'Golden Age' of late Victorian/ Edwardian cricket, is that style, technique and accepted 'orthodoxy' had become well established in both England and Australia.

Style had arrived, and shortly, one of the greatest exponents of stylish orthodoxy, Jack Hobbs, started his illustrious career. Australian opener and later writer, Jack Fingleton, was to write about the general Australian admiration for Hobbs, and in particular, of his pure style which "could not be bettered". I was fascinated to read in his autobiography, 'My Life Story', that as a boy Hobbs had practised with the use of a tennis ball and stump! He also mentioned that, similar to Bradman, he was self-taught. He wrote:

I helped my father at various odd jobs on the Jesus College ground during school holidays, such as scouting at the nets, and soon opportunities came of playing a sort of cricket with the college servants using a tennis ball and cricket stump for a bat and a tennis post for the wicket. This simple practice laid a wonderful foundation giving me a keen eye and developing the wrist strokes which I had seen in

BRADMAN REVISITED

*the college matches. Boy as I was, I tried to emulate
the same strokes and I was surprised at the number
of strokes I managed to make. That was the way I
became a natural batsman. The footwork came
automatically and the practice became a great
source of enjoyment when I recognised how
important everything was.*

Jack Hobbs (later to become Sir Jack Hobbs) scored
61,221 first class runs which included 197 centuries, both
records, and many judges look upon him as England's
greatest batsman. It is fascinating to discover that in
boyhood he played a similar game to Bradman and held
that simple exercise to be of fundamental importance to
his development. Bradman held similar views of his own
development.

Hobbs was an 'orthodox stylist' of whom Jack
Fingleton was to write in his 'Masters of Cricket 1958':

*Although figures indicate the greatness of Hobbs,
they don't convey the grandeur of his batting, his
faultless technique and the manner in which he
captivated those who could recognise and
analyse style. Australians who played against
him over the years believe cricket never
produced a more correct batsman than Hobbs.
But it is well to note Hobbs's claim that he never
had an hours coaching in his life. He was a self
taught cricketer observing, thinking and
executing for himself.*

SETTING THE SCENE

In Australia too, style, based on perceived orthodoxy, was a common denominator. Bradman was well aware of this and, late on in life during an interview, wryly remarked "cricket is the only game in the world you get marks for style". From the beginning he knew his style was very different to that of his contemporaries. He even accepted that aesthetically it would look "inferior" to the likes of Stan McCabe, of whom he was to write:

Here was a lovely player. He, like myself, was a country lad but his style was all polish and grace, for he came to the City early and gained experience on turf before his style was set.

Great players and stylists though they undoubtedly were, both Hobbs (Test average 56.94) and McCabe (Test average 48.21) were statistically well behind Bradman. To have them widely acclaimed as role models whilst Bradman is simply dismissed as unorthodox and not to be copied seems astonishing.

Marks for style are one thing but to allow style to rule the head without any 'scientific' back up is unsafe. Although there is still much more scientific work to be done, a start has been made and the signs so far indicate no practical disadvantages to the Bradman way of batting.

Due to his background and development as a cricketer, the views on batsmanship expressed by Don Bradman, both on tape and in his books, came from a totally different source of experience compared to those influenced by accepted orthodoxy. The latter are taught by written and spoken tenets based largely on the employment of a straight bat in making strokes. Bradman was not so restricted and taught himself how to control a fast-moving ball. The adoption of 'strokes' in an orthodox sense came later from experience. As has been shown, his style had fewer restrictions when it came to attacking stroke play and led him to write:

> *The basic technique of a straight bat is sound for defence. However, there should be all possible emphasis on attack, on the aggressive outlook, and if technique is going to prove the master of a player and not his servant, then it will not be doing its job.*

This indicates that while others were having difficulty coming to terms with his style, he clearly understood the workings and restrictions of 'orthodoxy'.

So much for style and its development since cricket became an international sport. Bradman was not the first 'unorthodox' player to make headline news, but his run scoring feats outclass all other players. It is time to have an in depth look into how he was seen at the time by both fellow cricketers and commentators. To his contemporaries it is clear from these many observations that his batting qualities and characteristics were appreciated. But there is a sense of confusion and some crucial misconceptions as to what it was that enabled him to do it.

4.

BRADMAN UNDER SCRUTINY

To begin to understand the bewilderment caused by Bradman from the 1930s onward as he continued to set new standards of consistent high scoring, it is necessary to read contemporary reports written by the experts of the day - both commentators and players. Their confusion is apparent and in some cases gave rise to some serious misunderstandings of just how these achievements were possible.

Mention has already been made of some of the reasons put forward to explain the Bradman phenomena covering both physical and mental aspects - and we can add to this some picturesque descriptions of his stroke play and demeanour. Above all, however, he was universally deemed 'unorthodox' and unique. More and more, the word 'genius' comes into use.

Eventually it was accepted that he was simply an unorthodox batting genius, and this seems to have been sufficient justification to not make an in-depth study of the technique he used to achieve such a status. That was just Bradman, and not to be copied. He appeared to do too many things 'wrong'! His 'genius' could be understood as a concept but it defied rational explanation. The accepted concept of orthodoxy could not be challenged by one man, no matter how outstanding.

BRADMAN REVISITED

In a more up-to-date context, it took some time for that great West Indian fast bowler Malcolm Marshall to have his unorthodox style of fast bowling accepted by mainstream coaching circles. Although always much admired, his style 'offended' the purists perhaps in a similar way to Bradman with his own stance and 'pick-up'. Perhaps the fact that recognition and acceptance eventually came for Marshall gives us some reason for hope that similar recognition will come for Bradman. There is, of course, a difference. Whereas statistically Marshall was one of a number of great fast bowlers, Don Bradman stood high and dry on his own pinnacle with no one else even close. The awe and confusion of his contemporaries is plain from their writings.

The Commentators' View

Writing in the London Evening News on the 28th April 1930, H. A. H. Carson wrote:

> *The main things which are taught in English cricket are the uplift of the bat, which should swing parallel to a line between the wicket and the use of the right foot in guarding the wicket. Bradman lifts his bat in the direction of point, and rarely moves his right foot to guard his stump.*

This article written at the beginning of the tour in 1930, but before his first knock against Worcestershire (in which he scored a double century), shows the degree of attention Bradman was already getting at the age of 21 after only two complete seasons in first class cricket. Before his first tour of England had started, he was noted to be unorthodox.

Writing in 'Cricket Up To Date' in 1931, writer E.D.H. Sewell wrote:

> *I do not admire Bradman's back play. It is quite unworthy of such a player. I guess since I have no other way of getting at the truth, that, roughly speaking, Bradman never plays right back on Australian wickets. He is an expert, if ugly, half cock player.*

Quite clearly the writer is confused by the Bradman way of batting. Although this was written early in Bradman's career he had already completed his triumphant 1930 tour of England and established a world record high score of 452.

In May 1938 Neville Cardus, arguably the most descriptive and picturesque of all cricket writers, wrote:

> *He scored a hundred in an hour with restraint. He played late on the whole, and his touch was so certain that we could almost feel that the blade of his bat was endowed with sight and was also prehensile. Now and again, true, he reached forward in a way not common for Bradman, who is a back foot player if ever there was one.*

This delightful cameo of a Bradman century is more concerned with the effect than the style and shows more than a little awe for the subject. Writing on an earlier occasion, during the 1934 tour, Cardus wrote of a dinner appointment he had with Bradman during the course of the Headingley Test. However, at the close of play on the first day the Aussies were 39-3, having dismissed England for 200. This caused Bradman to cancel his appointment with Cardus as he would need to make "200 at least" next day. Cardus then reminded Bradman that as during the previous tour he had made a triple century at Headingley, the law of averages was against him. Bradman replied: "I don't believe in the law of averages." He was as good as his word. Next day he scored 304!

Looking back on Bradman's career shortly after his retirement, cricket correspondent R.C. Robertson-Glasgow, writing in Wisden in 1949, wrote:

About his batting there was no style for style's sake. If there was to be any charm, that was for the spectator to find or miss. It was not Bradman's concern. His aim was for the making of runs, and he made them in staggering and ceaseless profusion. He seems to have eliminated error, to have perfected the mechanism of stroke.

This statement, coming from one of England's leading cricket writers, makes it seem all the more incredible that no one saw fit to fully investigate the style which produced such a result.

H. S. Altham and E. W. Swanton, in their joint venture 'History of Cricket', had this to say:

This photograph, taken in 1936, is an excellent study of Bradman's grip and stance - described by Jack Fingleton as unique. He adopted this position early as, in his own words, he "felt comfortable". On arriving in first class cricket he experimented in practice with the traditional approach but decided that for him it was more restrictive to attacking stroke play. This, therefore, is the way Bradman faced the world's bowlers during the whole of his career.

There does not appear to be any photographs of Bradman at play as a boy with golf ball and stump. It would be appropriate, if perhaps far-fetched, to believe that this 'fun' picture, in front of a large crowd, contains a coded message for the future!

This is a typical illustration of Bradman's method when driving through the off-side. The ball appears to have pitched wide of the off stump. Bradman, uncharacteristically, is at the pitch of the ball with head low and in line. Please note he is scoring in an area in which he feels he is more restricted!

The balance and co-ordinated control of this late cut shows Bradman using all of the crease.

The crowds roll up. Although at practice 'The Don' still demonstrates the concentration and poise of a perfect stroke. It was normal for Bradman to 'net' in front of large crowds. As this picture illustrates, he took his practice seriously.

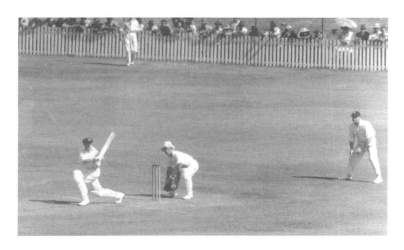

Bradman drives through the leg side off the front foot. The
thoughts of Wally Hammond, standing in the slips, can only
be guessed at. According to Hammond's own testimony he
had eliminated many of his favourite leg side shots
as he was, early in his career, led to believe they
offended cricket orthodoxy.

When these two great players were in their prime there was
no shortage of pundits who claimed Hammond was the better
batsman. This viewpoint was generally based on the idea that
Bradman in Australia batted on better wickets.

Below is a comparison of their averages covering all matches
during Bradman's tours of England when both players
were at their best.

1930	**Bradman**	36 innings	98.66
	Hammond	44 innings	53.47
1934	**Bradman**	27 innings	84.16
	Hammond	35 innings	76.32
1938	**Bradman**	26 innings	115.66
	Hammond	42 innings	75.27

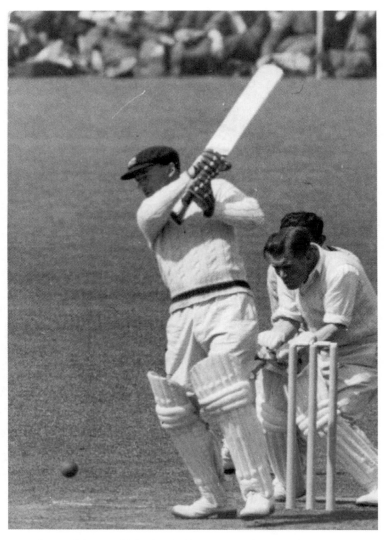

Bradman drives off the back foot. Note the positioning of his rear foot, which appears to point in the direction of the extra cover area. Bradman was flexible in his views on this controversial subject.

Bradman straight drives off the back foot. This time his rear
foot points straight past the bowler. It is clear that the position
of Bradman's rear foot, when driving, very much depended
upon where he was forcing the ball.

This type of stroke was the subject of discussion during Ray Martin's 87th birthday tribute to 'The Don':

Don Bradman: "My idea of a proper follow through after making a full-blooded drive."

Ray Martin: "Why don't we see this type of shot today with any of the great batsmen?"

Don Bradman: "I think it's because they are coached not to do it. It's a different technique."

SETTING THE SCENE

Genius defies analysis. But no one could watch a long innings by Bradman without realising some of his outstanding assets: a quite abnormally quick reaction commanding immediate obedience from a perfectly co-ordinated body to the message of an icily concentrated mind. Eyes, feet and wrists that see and work just a fraction quicker than the ordinary great players and enable him to meet with ease the most delayed threat of speed or swing and force ordinary length bowling almost where he willed through the gaps in the field. A repertoire of shots so elastic that those gaps always seemed to be there and yet so subordinate to his judgement that he could for hours cut out any that might involve unwarrantable risk. Add to this his immense determination, seemingly inexhaustible physical endurance and a genius for adapting his plans to the changing tactical situation. It may be that Bradman had not the sheer grace of Victor Trumper, the versatility on all wickets of Jack Hobbs, the annihilating unorthodoxy of Gilbert Jessop, but for the sheer ruthless efficiency no cricketer in the post-Grace era could compare with him.

E. W. Swanton is a byword as a cricket commentator in England. He is fulsome in his praise but is content to say that "genius defies analysis". Perhaps, but it does not mean that it should not be attempted. In his description there is no mention of technique. To E. W. Swanton the answer lies in his physical and mental attributes. On their own, these cannot account for Bradman's superiority. It still leaves unanswered the question 'how did he do it?'

Back in 1931 Eric Barbour wrote in the Sydney Mail:

Don Bradman is not an artist as were Victor Trumper, Ranji and Macartney, or even are Archie Jackson and Alan Kippax of the present generation. Bradman is a tradesman and a master tradesman.

Master tradesmen take years to perfect their art. There is no secret as to how they achieve their skills; their pathway is clearly marked. Bradman, it seems, invented his own trade which proved devastatingly successful, but no one seriously tried to understand how and why. He lacked the grace and style of other great players and perhaps therefore should not be copied for aesthetic reasons. Geniuses develop their own traits and are not meant to be role models.

In his autobiographical book 'Life Worth Living', C.B. Fry makes several references to Don Bradman. On one occasion he refers to "the great Don" and on another, "the phenomenal Don Bradman". He also suggests him alongside W. G. Grace and Ranjitsinhji as the three greatest batsmen. (But, of course, his book was written in 1939).

Although cricket figures prominently in his book, and he was an acknowledged academic and theorist, Fry does not involve himself at all with Bradman's technique. Despite being himself a pillar of orthodoxy, based on his own studies, to his credit he seemed to have few criticisms of 'unorthodox' players, and in fact was full of praise for 'Ranji', Gilbert Jessop and, of course, Don Bradman. I think this says a great deal for the cricket vision of C. B. Fry.

A correspondent for an Australian newspaper with the pseudonym 'Third Man' at the State match New South Wales versus Queensland in November 1933 had this to say of Don Bradman during his big partnership with W.A. Brown:

At the other end was Bradman. And if his partner shone in orthodoxy then the little champion positively sparkled in unorthodoxy. Balls that according to all the tenets of cricket should have been handled with a meticulous straight bat, were rudely despatched boundary-wards with a blade that artistically flashed across the line of flight without recording the suggestion that the user thereof was indulging in the 'cross-bat' so despised by his orthodox confreres of the willow.

Never was the mastery of Bradman more exemplified than in that single off-theory over of Thompson's when every ball was cracked to the unprotected leg, while the covers presented the appearance of an over starched paddock of flannel-clad fieldsmen.

Twenty six fours in a total of 200 was the result of uncanny placement, and of making openings where, if one relied on orthodox stroking, none really existed.

BRADMAN REVISITED

Most batsmen have their day making really big scores when things go for them, but Bradman made scoring double centuries more like a habit. He also made them quickly, and this account is fairly typical of a Bradman innings in the 1930s.

The Players' View

Shortly after the 1928/29 England tour of Australia, P.G.H. Fender, captain of Surrey and former England player, wrote a book containing this opinion of Bradman:

Bradman was one of the most curious mixtures of good and bad batting that I have ever seen. He made shots of the truly magnificent type, but never being able to avoid the really bad ones. If practice, experience and hard work enable him to eradicate faults he may well become a very good player. He will always be in the category of the brilliant but unsound ones.

He does not inspire one with any confidence that he desires to take the only course that will lead him to a fulfilment of that promise. He does not correct mistakes or look as if he were trying to do so.

Bradman was aware of this viewpoint, and when Australia came to play Surrey on the 1930 tour of England he gave Fender a reply - with his bat.

On the first day Bradman was at the crease early, the first wicket having fallen at 11. He played himself in carefully, his first 50 taking 90 minutes. In the next hour he doubled his score, and then went from 100 - 200 in 80 minutes. When rain stopped play five minutes early he was undefeated on 252 out of an Australian score of 379 for 5. The combined totals for the other batsmen, on a slow wicket, was 122 (five being extras).

It would have been interesting to have read Fender's thoughts as he lead his team from the field. Seldom in cricket has anyone been made to eat their own words more completely. It was early in Bradman's career when Fender passed this famous verdict but the general tone makes it difficult to sympathise with him. He was one of many who simply could not understand where such a batsman came from.

Kent and England stalwart Frank Woolley, writing in his book 'The King of Games', said:

Absolutely untaught, Bradman's success seems to make coaching a waste of time. Though he often plays with a cross bat, Bradman is the grandest living example for youngsters to copy in one particular. He really hits the ball.

Woolley, second only to Hobbs in numbers of first class career runs with 58,969 and seventh on the all-time century makers list with 145, is enthusiastic only up to a point. That "he really hits the ball" is apparently the only aspect of Bradman's batting for youngsters to copy. He does not analyse Bradman here but notes his 'unorthodoxy'. Coaching would indeed be a waste of time if it prevents young players developing naturally as did Bradman and Hobbs.

BRADMAN REVISITED

Bill O'Reilly, one of Australia's greatest spin bowlers, and no friend of Bradman, had no such problem with style or technique:

There's never been and never will be in my estimation a batsman as good as that fella. I don't care how many you like to pour into one - all the Chappells, the Borders and so on.

Forget them, they're just child's play compared with Bradman and I've seen them all. Bradman was a bloke whose ability with the bat was absolutely inconceivable. The Yanks talk about Babe Ruth and all that. To hell with Babe Ruth. This boy was a modern miracle.

O'Reilly was a teammate of Bradman at New South Wales before Bradman left to join South Australia at the end of season 1933/34. Thereafter he still played with Bradman for Australia on many occasions. They were widely different in character and at times during their careers O'Reilly's antipathy towards Bradman was the subject of much comment. His praise of Bradman is the more to be respected as an impartial opinion of Bradman's talent.

Dennis Compton, who played in three series against Bradman, said in 1980:

Bradman had a marvellous way of getting into position quicker than any batsman I have ever seen, played the ball very late and was never off balance or stretching out of control.

SETTING THE SCENE

Compton, himself one of cricket's greats, seems to see Bradman's secret as based on footwork, concentration and balance. A respected view, but Compton would be the first to admit there was more to it than that. In his autobiography of Dennis Compton, Peter West tells an amusing story of the second Test at Sydney in December 1946. Bradman was approaching yet another 200 and Compton, a useful spin bowler in those days, had been instructed by Hammond to keep Bradman quiet by bowling wide of the off stump to an offside field. Despite this stratagem the leg-side boundary continued to be lashed. An irate Hammond accosted Compton, who replied; "I heard you skipper, I haven't yet pitched one less than two feet wide of the off-stump." Allowing for storyteller's license, we get the message. Through the years, better bowlers than Compton would have recognised his problem.

Jim Laker was just such a bowler. His cricket career was delayed by the war, and when he faced the Australians in 1948, he was still a comparatively inexperienced spin bowler. He played in the famous Headingley Test in which Australia scored 404 in less than a day's play on a worn pitch and didn't get a wicket when many people thought he could be the match winner. Bradman scored an unbeaten 173 and it was an experience Laker never forgot.

He had something of a revenge in 1956 when taking a record 19 wickets in the Old Trafford Test, finishing the series with 46 victims - another record. But it was the 1948 season which lived in his mind, and Don Bradman in particular. Altogether that year he played in six matches against Australia during which Bradman scored 868 runs at an average of 108.5, including four centuries. Not once did Laker, who became one of England's greatest ever spinners, get his wicket. Small wonder he was later to write: "He's the only batsman I ever bowled to who gave me an inferiority complex."

Maurice Tate of Sussex and one of England's leading bowlers in the 1920s advised Bradman during the 1928/29 series in Australia: "You'll have to learn to play with a straighter bat before you come to England." This serious misreading of Bradman's talent almost ranks alongside the Fender quote earlier in this chapter.

Wilfred Rhodes of Yorkshire has claims to being England's greatest ever all-rounder. Between 1898 and 1930 he took 4188 first class wickets at an average of 16.71 - which is still a record. During this period he scored 39,802 runs at an average of 30.83 including 58 centuries. Writing in 1935, just five years after finishing playing, he wrote:

Bradman is an example of Test Match Temperament par excellence. His confidence is supreme. No matter how you bowl at him he seems to be able to place the ball just where he likes. He makes the bowling suit his batting - which is real cricket and the right spirit of cricket. It would have been a great sight to see Bradman matching his eye and skill against Sid Barnes's clever bowling - the greatest batsman and the greatest bowler.

SETTING THE SCENE

In commenting on Bradman's spirit, Rhodes is expressing a Yorkshireman's heartfelt admiration for Bradman's aggressive intent, as well as his skill. He does not seem concerned with cause - only effect.

Most of the quotes from both famous players and commentators have a theme, - wonderment and admiration tinged almost with disbelief. The few critical quotes were made early in Bradman's career when the writers had no way of knowing that he would maintain the phenomenal standard he had set himself. No one however suggests that Bradman should be studied, let alone copied. He was always considered a man apart.

In season 1931/32 South Africa toured Australia with a young fast bowler named A. J. Bell. At the end of the tour he wrote a full account of the impression Bradman made on himself and his team-mates. It reads as fresh now as it did then and vividly brings back the aura which already surrounded Bradman in the cricket world after only four years in the game.

Bowling to Bradman

A.J. Bell, the Springbok fast bowler, had a great many opportunities of studying the great Australian batsman. He bowled to Bradman in seven matches, often for an entire day without once getting his wicket. "Most people in South Africa," he says, "seem to be under the impression that Bradman is a great forward player. This is quite erroneous. He is the finest back player any of us have ever seen." The following is an excerpt from Bell's book:

BRADMAN REVISITED

You never hear the name Bradman in Australia. He is simply, 'Our Don'.

There were thousands of cricketing enthusiasts at the quayside, all of whom greeted us with the usual formula: 'Wait till Our Don gets you'. In Sydney we were received by the New South Wales Cricket Association and there we met many old friends of South African cricketers including Jack Gregory, Sam Ryder, Bert Oldfield, Charlie McCartney, and dozens of others. Of course we were most anxious to get a glimpse of Don Bradman.

Imagine our surprise on seeing a tiny fellow in a neat grey suit, and then finding him to be the redoubtable Don Bradman.

Enough has been written about him to fill a book. But off the field he has a remarkable personality, more especially when one considers that four years ago he was a nonentity in the small township of Bowral and now is easily the most magnetic figure in the world of cricket. He is a good conversationalist, obviously out to learn all that he can, and he gives one the impression of being an astute business man. You feel when you talk to him that he is probing you. His eyes are never still. You feel that he will not be satisfied until he knows all about your bowling and your batting. You can see that he makes a close study of cricket and has unusual powers of concentration.

SETTING THE SCENE

He does not talk about himself to any marked degree. He takes all his amazing performances as a matter of course. He tells you quite candidly that he is determined to better his previous records.

Our first encounter with Don was on the Sydney Oval when we played New South Wales for the first time. Neville Quinn had been left out of this game in order to be a surprise packet for the first Test. Morkel and I had a few overs at Don, and he did not impress us as anything out of the ordinary. Quentin McMillan and Cyril Vincent then took over the bowling. For about 80 minutes Don put up a very scratchy display, finally ending his innings at 30, caught and bowled by McMillan.

Naturally we were all somewhat elated and felt that we more or less had the measure of him. On the last day of the match we declared, leaving New South Wales 450 to get to win. We disposed of Wendill Bill, and Bradman came in. McMillan promptly was given the ball. But this was not the same Bradman. McMillan's first ball was a good length, fast spinner. Don ran about five yards up the pitch and cracked it like a bullet past mid-on to the pickets (the boundary). *After this we were entertained to one of the most magnificent exhibitions of footwork any of us had ever seen.*

Don never allowed McMillan to pitch the ball anywhere near a decent length, but hit it on the full-toss all the time. This rather changed our views about the little wizard. However, we put our faith in Neville Quinn. He bowled over the wickets in Australia, making the ball do a little bit either way.

Arriving at Brisbane we soon realised that Don had shown them the way of dealing with McMillan. The story of the first Test match is simply this - Bradman was dropped twice before he had scored 20, and on both occasions off Neville Quinn. In Brisbane Don broke Trumper's record against the 1911 Springboks, giving a magnificent display of forceful hitting.

Most people in South Africa seem to be under the impression that Bradman is a great forward player. This is quite erroneous. He is the finest forcing back player any of us have ever seen. To slow bowling he uses his feet marvellously, placing the ball when and where he likes. Against fast and medium bowling he does not score at quite the same phenomenal rate, but employs entirely different tactics.

One pitches a good length on his leg stump and the ball gathers another coat of paint off the pickets of the fine leg boundary, and one's bowling average increases by another four. If you bowl the ball just short of a length on the off pin he takes great pains over his shot and is content to push it down the gully for a single, or just out of reach of the unfortunate fielder.

We tried for four and a half months to get him caught in the slips by bowling short just outside off stump. His wonderful placing and command over the ball made life absolutely untenable for gully and point.

When batting Bradman always seems, to the weary bowler at any rate, to assume a sort of cynical grin, which rather reminds me of the Sphinx. We tried to shift that grin; but I think Neville Quinn was the only one of us successful, and that was in the third Test at Melbourne when Cameron caught him for two.

His command of shots is nothing short of marvellous. He seems to know just what kind of ball you are going to bowl and where you are going to bowl it. He makes up his mind in a flash and does not hit the ball to the fielder as a great many do, but places it just out of reach and grins cheerfully.

To bowl to him is heart-breaking. He takes risks but never seems to pay the cost which his temerity deserves. His hook shot is incredible. He steps right back on to the wicket (one does not see much wicket when he is batting) and cracks the ball plumb in the middle of the bat about 99 times out of 100. When he does mistime the ball, and that is very infrequently, the ball does not shoot up into the air and fall into the avaricious wicket-keeper's hands, but drops harmlessly on the ground. This is due to the fact that with every shot he plays he intends the ball to hit the ground just a couple of yards from his feet. In all his shots he seems to turn the wrist over so that on the completion of the stroke the face of his bat is towards the ground.

BRADMAN REVISITED

The remarkable thing about the little wizard is that while fast and medium bowling is fresh he contents himself by never attempting to score in front of the wicket but glides the ball down the leg side or hits it like a bullet between point and third man. This last shot of his is, I think, his favourite.

If I ever play against Don Bradman again I think the best thing to do will be to bowl the fast full toss straight for the top of the off-stump. That seems to be the only ball he is content to pat back to the bowler. On second thoughts, however, he probably would work out a counter-offensive and land it up against the pickets in his usual manner!

Bradman's running between the wickets was an eye-opener. I have seen him make nearly 200 runs in one day and at the end of the day seem to the weary bowlers to run faster than when he began at 12 o'clock. He runs for everything. He hits the ball just short of cover-point and runs a quick single. Cover-point comes in and he then places it just out of reach of his left hand. He does this to every fielder in the team.

Consequently, when Don comes in nobody knows where to stand, and they pray fervently either that he'll go out, or that six o'clock will hurry up.

Another remarkable thing about Bradman is that he never seems to perspire. Our bowlers used to get through three or four shirts a day, but Don comes out in an immaculate silk shirt at noon and at six o'clock it is still an immaculate silk shirt.

SETTING THE SCENE

At Adelaide the temperature was 108 in the shade. Don was in the course of making 299. We were all just about exhausted, but Don - he was as fresh as a new pin. The only sign of his 180 runs was a tiny little damp spot in the middle of his back.

Apart from Don's actual play in the field he is looked upon as a national hero in Australia. He is easily the greatest drawing-card in the cricket world of to-day: probably the greatest of all time. We had an instance of this in the third Test at Melbourne. Don was 97 not out on the previous night. We started the next day at noon. Old players and officials of the Melbourne cricket ground told us that they had never seen such a queue to get in the members' gate. At the commencement of play there were 32,000 people.

Needless to say Don dispatched the first ball for three, making his 100. If I remember he got 160 odd and lost his wicket just prior to the luncheon adjournment. On the re-opening of play at 1.45 the crowd numbered about 20,000, which goes to prove that 12,000 at least only came to the ground to see Don get his century.

As regards his fielding I saw both Andrews and Pellew in the Australian side that played in South Africa in 1919 and they were considered to be among the world's best. I think it only fair to say that Bradman outshines any outfield in the world.

His running is phenomenal. If he sees a ball travelling towards the boundary he suddenly starts off after what seems to be a certain four, and to everybody's amazement he stops it with his foot just on the boundary.

He then throws it back in much the same way as 'Tupps' Owen-Smith. One of Don's idiosyncrasies is that no matter whether the batsmen are still running or are stationary in their crease he still pelts the ball straight at the wicket. If throwing square to the wicket he hits it from the boundary once in three times.

Our running between the wickets was very bad and to some degree I think Don Bradman was responsible. One never knew how quickly he was capable of disarranging the wickets from a boundary throw.

His ground fielding was exceptionally good: but the Australians who toured England in 1930 aver that he is not a very safe catch. Whether this is so we really never had a chance of observing. As in his batting his judgment of the pace of the ball in the field is wonderful.

He is the perfect example for the budding cricketer. He neither smokes nor drinks. He keeps reasonably early hours and looks after himself very carefully. He does a course of physical training, and combines it with wrestling. As regards the bogy of golf he seems rather to explode that theory. He is very fond of the game, plays off about eight and wins various competitions. So much for golf affecting the strokes of a batsman!

He plays the piano remarkably well, and plays most tunes he is asked either from ear or music. His only downfall against the South Africans was at a charity meeting when Eric Dalton beat him in a ping-pong match.

To sum up Don is rather a difficult job. He has done enough to make 20 average men swollen-headed. And yet that is the last thing one could accuse him of. He has a queer way of talking about himself. To all appearances he is batting well, and yet he will tell you quite candidly that he never bats well on the day following a big score. We could never detect a flaw in his batting.

He is one of the most magnetic personalities I have ever met in the course of my cricket career. He speaks with a strong Australian accent. Quite definitely he is an Australian. He is proud of it and Australia is proud of him. Whether he has reached the zenith of his powers cannot be said. But I think Alan Kippax hit the nail on the head when he said to me:

'If Don played for the West Indies they would be the leading cricketing country. If he played for New Zealand they would be the leading cricketing country. If he played for England they would be the leading cricketing country. If he played for South Africa they would be the leading cricketing country.'

And at that I leave it.

A.J. Bell's account of the effect Bradman had on opposing teams can hardly be more evocative. It is probably true to say that nobody else in cricket history came near to having such an effect. It is also worth noting that Bell is another who does not concern himself with style - only effect. The 'runs on the board' and the rate at which they were scored were all that concerned him. In this pragmatic appreciation he joins renowned writers such as Robertson-Glasgow and E.W. Swanton, previously quoted.

Their admiration of Bradman is fulsome and uncomplicated. No serious attempt is made to analyse the style and technique behind his unique achievements, instead, they attribute his success, in varying degrees, to physical and mental causes.

It is well to remind ourselves of how Bradman shaped up in this respect. We have already seen how tests conducted at Adelaide University showed Bradman's eyesight to be slightly below average, and that he missed the whole of season 1934/35 through ill health. When he should have been in his prime as a batsman the war intervened, as it did with so many other players approaching their best years.

In December 1940 a specialist again examined Bradman's eyes and found they had deteriorated in recent years and were surprisingly poor. At the age of 32 Bradman was discharged from the army in 1941 with fibrositis. This affected the muscles of his back and had been a long-standing problem. During the whole of his career, worries about Bradman's health were surprisingly frequent. When he was fit, like all short wiry athletes, his reflexes were of course excellent. But this alone cannot begin to explain his pre-eminence.

SETTING THE SCENE

As far as mental strength is concerned, Bradman was, without doubt, very well equipped. Many great cricketers have enjoyed similar mental strength. It's part of the recipe for greatness. There is no reason to suppose that Bradman had any advantage here except perhaps in one crucial aspect - concentration. We have touched on this in an earlier chapter and it is so important it will come up again.

If it wasn't mainly physical or mental, where does it leave us? There is really only one way to go. Having looked at him through the eyes of both commentators and players it is time to look in more detail at what Bradman himself had to say. There was nothing secretive or mysterious about him, he explained his approach in great detail.

The Bradman View

When first learning to play cricket as schoolboys, most youngsters are encouraged to adopt an 'orthodox' stance. Parents, teachers, or perhaps coaches will teach them the accepted techniques which produce a batting style perceived as orthodox.

Due to his circumstances as a boy, Don Bradman arrived at his batting style in a manner quite different to this. His development was not affected by any constraints of pre-judged techniques. He set himself the simple goal of controlling a fast-moving ball. In the beginning this happened to be a golf ball, using a cricket stump as a bat. His grip on the stump was the most suitable for him to achieve his objective. All his movements became instinctive and quickly habitual. When he was older, using a proper bat and ball, his basic method of ball control did not change.

Bradman's batsmanship cannot be properly assessed and understood without realising that his reasoning and explanations are born from this unusual development. He uses a different, much more fundamental, cricket language:

> *I cannot emphasise too much my belief that 'concentration' and 'watching the ball' are of greater importance than all the theories. They could be the last words before anyone goes in to bat.*

This would sound glib coming from someone else, but Bradman was not a man prone to wasting words. They assume an even deeper significance when viewed together with C. B. Fry's previously quoted discourse on batting concentration.

His views on coaching young players are typically forthright:

> *It is a mistake to fog a boy's mind with a multiplicity of complicated instructions which means he forgets the much more important and simple basic principals.*
>
> *Too many players fail because their thoughts are concentrated on where their left elbow is or where something else is instead of hitting the ball.*

These words were written more than 50 years ago and are perhaps even more applicable today when technique with structured strokes are part of the production line approach to coaching young players (as evidenced in the MCC Masterclass coaching video).

There is one aspect of Bradman's batting which was never understood and this relates to his early movement.

All commentators, including players, were impressed by Bradman's stillness at the crease as the bowler made his approach. Jack Fingleton has already been quoted in the introduction and is so important that it's worth repeating:

Bradman's batting stance is unique. His bat touched the ground between his feet and not behind them like every other batsman and photograph I have seen. He stood perfectly still as the bowler approached, the end of his bat did not act as an escape conductor for energy with that nervous tap tap tap on the pitch, so common to most batsmen as the bowler ran to deliver the ball. Bradman at the wicket was completely at ease and at rest until the ball began its apologetic advance towards him.

One of England's top commentators over many years, John Arlott, wrote:

He stood at the crease perfectly immobile until the ball was on its way, then his steps flowed like quicksilver out of trouble or into position to attack.

Sir Pelham Warner went further:

BRADMAN REVISITED

It is strikingly apparent how absolutely still Bradman stands until the ball is halfway down the pitch. Then follows a lightening movement of his feet and the bat, and the ball crashes into the crowd.

All Bradman commentators were unanimous in stating that Bradman made no movement until after the ball left the bowler's hand. Bradman himself contradicts this and, explaining how some batsmen seem to have more time than others, in his book 'The Art of Cricket', wrote:

One cause may be the relative moments at which different batsmen start to move their feet and lift their bats. In theory one would make out a case for standing still and not moving the bat until you see the ball in the air and know where it is pitching.

In practice this doesn't happen and I am all in favour of the batsman starting to lift his bat and make a preliminary movement with his feet before the ball is actually delivered.

It saves a precious fraction of a second and appears to serve the same purpose as the preliminary waggle before starting your swing at golf. It's not part of the swing but it gets you started.

Bradman is clearly saying that his bat and feet had started their movements before, and not after, the ball had left the bowler's hand. Not an easy thing to detect in those days when instant action replays and slow motion analysis were not even distant dreams.

Even today, with all the advantages of modern technology, how often in football does a linesman flag for offside, only for slow motion replays to show the 'flagged' player to be well onside when the ball was last played? The linesman's problem of course is that he cannot watch two different areas at precisely the same time. So it was (and is) with cricket.

Watching the precise moment a ball leaves the bowler's hand while at the same time attempting to note the exact time the batsman reacts is difficult even with television close-ups behind the bowler's arm. So this crucial element of Bradman's batting was missed by all. Nobody, it seems, took notice of what he actually wrote about it. Without this early movement, batting loses its effectiveness. In Bradman's case, his ability to play every stroke from the same early batting motion was fundamental to his superb co-ordination and is crucial to understanding his batsmanship.

Bradman also had very clear views on the straight bat and 'back-lift'. He wrote:

The basic technique of the straight bat is sound for defence. However, there should be all possible emphasis on attack, on the aggressive outlook, and if technique is going to prove the master of a player and not his servant then it will not be doing its job.

BRADMAN REVISITED

He continued:

The straight back-lift has greater limitations in versatile stroke-making.

Bradman obviously considered his style, with its initial outward bat movement, allowed additional scope when it came to scoring runs.

As far as coaching was concerned Bradman believed that the freedom to develop naturally should be the starting point. Again, in his book 'The Art of Cricket', he wrote:

Coaching should deal with what to do with the ball not so much as how to do it. The coach must have sufficient intelligence not to be dogmatic but to discern what method is best for his pupil.

This highlights the difference in how Bradman thought about the game and stems directly from his early training where control of the ball was everything. It also recalls to mind Walter Hammond's much quoted statement; "A good shot is one that controls the ball". To this end Bradman wrote:

I would council every boy who is interested in batting to play with a ball at every opportunity. Whether it is a golf ball, tennis ball, baseball or any other kind does not matter. It will help train the eye and co-ordinate brain, eye and muscle. There is nothing better than constant playing with a ball.

74

SETTING THE SCENE

Reports on a Bradman innings when he was in his prime in the 1930s unfailingly refer to his ability to place the ball wide of fieldsmen at will on either side of the wicket. As E.W. Swanton put it, "gaps always seem to be there". His control over a cricket ball was (and is) unequalled. Just as significant he never appeared to commentators as though he was taking any risks as he kept the scoreboard racing along. Neville Cardus wrote: "He scored a hundred in an hour with restraint". All the images framed are of a man in total control of himself and the bowling.

All great batsmen have their purple patches but no one comes close to sustaining them in the manner of Bradman. So how was he able to do it? The main reason is not physical or mental but simply that the style and co-ordination he developed for himself allowed it. That, and the constant practice that all sporting 'greats' need to sustain their performance. Quoting again from 'The Art of Cricket', he wrote:

> *Eventually a batsman should reach a stage when his judgement at whether to play forward or back becomes instinctive rather than deliberate. The sight of the ball seems to trigger off a corresponding reaction so that movement becomes almost a habit.*

In his prime, Bradman had evolved and perfected a style of batting which became a habit. The smooth early movement of each shot was the same. Habits are not tiring. This explains why, to the astonishment of all commentators, Bradman could leave the field after a big innings, stretching over anything up to six hours, and not appear to be tired. Sometimes he would even leave the field of play after a long innings breaking into a trot as he did so.

No one doubts that Bradman was a batting genius, but can his method be copied successfully? Is it better for young players not to be aware of this method - if so, why? Could it actually be better than the orthodoxy which has prevailed during the whole of the 20th century? I believe that this book will provide the answers to these and other questions.

5.

THE SCIENTIFIC APPROACH

Applying new technology to cricket did not occur to me until, by chance, I came across an article in our local newspaper, The Liverpool Daily Post. To my great surprise I learned that soccer countries of South America - Brazil, Argentina, Uruguay and Peru - were employing the specialised skills of Liverpool's John Moores University to study the movement and balance of their footballers.

It was clear that the University's Centre for Sport and Exercise department had a worldwide reputation, with this particular project handled by Professor Tom Reilly.

If they were able to make such a study for football my thoughts turned to the possibility of a similar study for cricket. With this in mind I made a telephone call and was put in touch with Professor Lees of the same department.

I briefly outlined my thoughts on batting movement to Professor Lees with particular reference to the different approach of Don Bradman, and was delighted with his open-minded reception. This telephone conversation resulted in my meeting Professor Lees at the University where we agreed to a broad approach to the subject of batting. This covered three aspects:

1. Mental and Physical.
2. Technique.
3. The motion required to perform the technique.

BRADMAN REVISITED

Points 2 and 3 would be studied both from the orthodox stance and technique, and from the very different Bradman style. It worked as follows:

Sixteen electronic sensors were attached to various parts of the body and arms with three on the bat. Six fixed position cameras were then used to produce three-dimensional computer images for comparison between the Bradman style and the conventional style in making a whole range of strokes. The quality of the high-speed cameras allowed analysis at 240 samples per second as opposed to 25 samples per second available using a normal video camera.

Professor Lees' interest is in sportsmen in general and without particular favour. Towards the end of my first meeting with him we had a brief look at Bradman's instructional video 'How to Play Cricket'. Interestingly he quickly drew attention to Bradman's use of the hips when generating power and executing his strokes. This aspect had been noted in other outstanding sportsmen. When Nick Faldo was asked his view on Tiger Woods' hitting power he drew immediate attention to his use of the hips. A study made of fast bowler Frank Tyson also showed up to 40% of pace came from transfer of the hips. This suggests that a general study of hip movement might prove valuable to batsmen.

When Professor Lees produced a report on the preliminary investigation I furnished the details to local journalist Michael Handley, who featured extracts from it on Tuesday 25th April in Liverpool's Daily Post. The result was astonishing. There was immediate worldwide interest with coverage on TV, internet, radio and newspapers. If I had any lingering doubts about the cricket world's continued interest in Bradman, here was the answer. Professor Lees found himself centre stage. However, he did point out that his report was a preliminary one and that there was much work that could be done - if there was proper financial backing. The nature of the work was highly technical, time-consuming and, of course, using the University's much-in-demand hi-tech equipment. Even so, some of the leading newspapers gave extensive coverage and the following are extracts from their subsequent calls to Professor Lees.

Russell Jenkins, The Times, 26th April 2000:

SCIENCE BACKS THE WILD SIDE
OF CRICKET GENIUS

Although the great Australian terrorised English bowlers for several decades, his stance and skewed backlift were considered to be too unorthodox to be used in coaching manuals.

Sports scientists have concluded that following computer analysis Sir Don Bradman's batting technique could be a good role model after all and that youngsters will not go far wrong emulating the Australian sporting legend. More extensive analysis may eventually suggest that young English cricketers will perform better if they are not taught to eradicate their idiosyncrasies early in their development.

BRADMAN REVISITED

Tim Knowles, The Daily Mail, April 26th 2000:

WHY THE DON WAS RIGHT NOT TO PLAY WITH A STRAIGHT BAT

He is widely regarded as the greatest batsman of all time. But while Sir Donald Bradman's scores made him the envy of cricketers the world over, his batting style has always been frowned upon by the establishment. Now scientists have proved what lovers of cricket statistics have long known, there is nothing wrong with the legendary Australian's style in front of the stumps.

Professor Lees said, 'There is no evidence that the Bradman technique disadvantaged the batsman, Bradman was an exceptionally talented person who developed a technique which suited the skill and that combination was extremely powerful.'

Nigel Bunyan, The Daily Telegraph, April 26th 2000:

COMPUTER HITS ON THE SECRET OF BRADMAN'S STYLE

Since his heyday, coaches around the world have shunned his unconventional approach, instead raising generations of cricketers to favour a straight back-lift. Now scientists in the biomechanics department of Liverpool's John Moores University are working on research that could rewrite the cricketing manuals.

SETTING THE SCENE

Scientists found that, while a batsman using either technique would actually play the ball with a straight bat, the Bradman technique had two advantages: firstly, it allowed the player to delay the moment he decided which shot to play and, secondly, its forward motion automatically put him on his toes.

Such advantages provide a batsman with only an extra split-second of decision making and balance, but they could at least begin to explain Bradman's superiority at the crease. 'The research we've done so far has been fascinating,' said Professor Lees. 'But before it can reach its potential a lot more has to be done and for that we need financing. We haven't, for example, looked at how a player's back-lift is co-ordinated with a player's foot movement.'

Phillip Derriman, The Sydney Morning Herald, April 28th 2000:

HALF A CENTURY LATER IT SEEMS THE BOWRAL BOY'S TECHNIQUE IS WORTH COPYING AFTER ALL

There is sweet irony in the fact that a recent move to recognise Sir Donald Bradman's technique as a model for young batsmen throughout the world to follow should have originated in, of all places, England.

The English view in Sir Don's own day was that he was plainly unorthodox: that his amazing

81

BRADMAN REVISITED

success was achieved not because of, but in spite of, his batting methods. The idea underlying all this was that he was a kind of freak of nature, a one-off marvel for whom ordinary principles did not apply.

The following week Damian Ryan and his technician from Australia's Channel 9 TV travelled from London to John Moores University to meet Professor Lees and myself in order to put together a news item to be shown on Australian TV. After some filming I invited them to my home and the 'Bradman Room' - where I keep all my research notes and archive films. Appropriately we finished viewing a video of the Don in action.

To my great delight Damian was kind enough to forward a copy of the finished tape he produced with the comment that "the story was a hit".

Australian and English radio were also involved, interviewing both Professor Lees and myself, and subsequent internet interest was shown by India's national newspaper The Hindu. More than 50 years after he finished playing, the cricket world, it seems, is just as hungry as ever to find out how Bradman did it. I hope by the time the reader completes this book he will be satisfied that the big secret was really no secret at all, because Bradman revealed and demonstrated every aspect of his development and method in his books, booklets and demonstration video.

What Bradman's style has been unable to achieve is to break down the 'barriers' of orthodox thinking and application when it comes to batsmanship.

SETTING THE SCENE

Since starting my research I have at various times communicated with the MCC at Lord's and, as some initial interest was shown, I sent them a copy of Professor Lees' report from John Moores University. Lord's were kind enough to acknowledge receipt, but I have had no further communication on the subject.

Being English, I have always felt that attempting to explain Bradman to Australians is akin to intruding into a private family affair. This uneasiness has proved to be unfounded and I cannot speak too highly of the friendly and responsive attitude shown by all the Australians with whom I have been in contact, including the great encouragement of a letter written by Sir Donald himself.

In the meantime neuroscientists at the Universities of Oxford and Sussex have been conducting some extremely interesting studies into eyesight and judgement when applied to stroke-making with a cricket bat. This is basically concerned with how much time a batsman has and how long he keeps his eye on the ball. The report was summarised by Helen Briggs, BBC Online, Monday 20th November 2000, and is stimulating enough to be quoted in full. Although it is perhaps too early to offer firm views on scientific investigations, there is clearly much to learn from harnessing and developing new technology. It is to be hoped that more money can be made available to assist the Universities in their investigations.

BRADMAN REVISITED

Helen Briggs, BBC Online,
Monday 20th November 2000:

SCIENCE'S SURPRISING VIEW OF CRICKET

The old adage 'keep your eye on the ball' may not be appropriate advice for cricket players - at least, for some of the time they are standing at the crease.

Scientists have found that the best batsmen actually take their eyes off the ball before knocking it for six.

And the longer they are able not to watch the ball, the better players they are likely to make.

The researchers studied three cricketers of varying ability and found that the one professional player in the group would follow the ball as it left the bowler's hand but then quickly shift his gaze to the predicted bounce point. This allowed the player to better prepare himself for the shot.

Two amateurs carried out a similar pattern of eye movements but watched the path of the ball for longer.

The study was carried out by neuroscientists at the Universities of Oxford and Sussex, UK.

Co-researcher Michael Land said: 'I think batsmen will be horrified to hear they take their eyes off the ball. It certainly surprised us.'

The researchers concluded that a player's eye movement strategy contributed to the skill of their game.

SETTING THE SCENE

Professionals were also better at estimating how fast the ball would travel after it had bounced, they said.

And science seems to support the testimony of top batsmen about the need for early information about the curve that a ball will follow.

'In a perfect world, you will see the ball early and play it late,' former England cricket player Geoff Boycott is quoted as saying.

Ex-England captain and left-hander David Gower has said: 'The key to playing all strokes is to see quickly the line and length of the ball and to move early into the appropriate position.'

Of the two amateurs in the study, one was judged a 'good amateur' and the other regarded as a 'Sunday morning enthusiast'.

Each wore special cameras mounted on their heads during sessions in the nets when balls were delivered at 80 kilometres (50 miles) per hour from a bowling machine.

The camera recorded the view from the batsman's left eye and the direction of their gaze.

When the videos were analysed, the players all showed the same basic pattern of events. None of them watched the ball continuously.

They all followed the predicted path of the ball for a fraction of a second after it left the bowler's hand.

They then moved their gaze rapidly below the ball to watch for the site where it was likely to bounce.

They fixated again on the ball as it bounced and followed its upward curve for a short time afterwards.

The best batsman had the shortest delay between the ball's release and moving his eyes to where he calculated it would bounce. This enabled him to prepare for his shot.

These rules apply to fast and medium-speed bowling where the ball can travel up to 150 kilometres (93 miles) per hour. Slow bowling, where spin rather than speed is deployed, is a different ball game.

The research is reported in the journal 'Nature Neuroscience'.

N.B. I have quoted these findings in full in the belief that they are directly related to Bradman's boyhood game and its ultimate effect upon his instinctive judgement.

PART 2

Bradman's Secret

BRADMAN REVISITED

IN THE FIRST SECTION we have briefly shown how cricket developed through the early nineteenth century onwards and, in doing so, gradually established for itself a recognised 'orthodoxy' based broadly on a pendulum motion of the bat - with the first priority, defence of the wicket.

We hope we have also shown the bewilderment Bradman caused as, over a 20-year career, he proceeded to re-write the record books using a very different style of batting to that considered 'orthodox'.

Having thus established the existence of two totally different batting methods in terms of development, mentality and technique, the following pages seek to analyse Bradman's style in depth and compare it with that perceived as orthodox.

We have also shown that the scientific laboratory studies so far completed give us no reason to think that orthodoxy has any advantages. On the contrary, we have every reason to believe our study has shown the converse to be the case.

There really never was a Bradman 'secret' as such. He wrote enough coaching material and was there to be studied in person over a 20-year span. The truth is, for a number of reasons which will be examined in more detail in this section, nobody seriously tried to find out how he did it.

1.

GRIP AND STANCE

The trademark Bradman image at the crease shows a relaxed stance, his bat resting naturally between his feet with the face closed. A closer look will show that both hands are held close together with the thumb and the first finger of each hand forming an inverted 'V' with the insertion of the bat handle down the rear of the bat. It is obvious that from this position the initial movement of the bat will be away from the body and not backwards. At this point it is also well to note that Bradman always used a light short-handled bat (2lb 2oz - 2lb 7oz).

Standing in this manner enabled Bradman to commence all his strokes from a position of perfect balance. In this respect, C.B. Fry explained the crucial importance of balance in his in-depth analysis of batting:

> *What is required is not a position which it is natural to get into, but one which it is natural to get out of, in order to pass rapidly into strokes upon which even the so called 'genius' has to spend much time and trouble before he masters them.*

Throughout his career Bradman's grip and stance caused much controversy. However, the simple fact is that it was because of this that Bradman's batting motion and footwork was fundamentally different to more orthodox players. The latter commence a straighter backlift from a bat positioned, to varying degrees, behind the rear foot with the face of the bat open.

From the strictly orthodox standpoint Bradman's grip and stance would appear to be wrong. One cannot however expect the same grip to be used for stances and 'backlift' which are very different. In his book, 'The Art of Cricket', Bradman had this to say on the subject:

> *I allowed my bat to rest on the ground between my feet simply because it was a comfortable and natural position.*
>
> *It is regarded as more orthodox to teach a pupil to rest his bat just behind his right toe. This position encourages a straighter back-lift, is perhaps sounder for defensive play, but, I feel it has greater limitations in versatile stroke-making.*

Bradman tells us in this statement that his own level of performance could not have been achieved had he adopted a more orthodox approach. It is important that the reader recognises the significance of this statement.

Geoffrey Boycott, who has kindly shown an interest in my research, told me that in regard to grip, he too preferred the 'V' of his lower hand to be in line with the insertion of the bat handle, and also went on to say that Len Hutton used a similar grip.

2.

EARLY MOVEMENT

This feature of Bradman's play has been more misunderstood than any other.

There are two aspects to be considered. The first is 'When?' - at what point in time did he start to move his bat? The second is 'How?' - what direction did his bat take?

We have already quoted Bradman himself on his early bat movement and illustrated how most, if not all, Bradman-watchers got it wrong. We have tried to establish the image of a man standing perfectly at ease and absolutely still at the crease as the bowler makes his approaching run. Sometime during that split second when the bowler arrives at the crease and begins his action, Bradman starts to react.

Not only did he commence his batting movement before the ball was released, but his unique grip and stance induced a smooth continuous motion of the wrists, arms, shoulders and bat through to the completion of his selected stroke. His initial bat movement being away from his body, rather than straight back, meant that he was taken naturally onto the balls of both feet, the perfect position of balance for moving either forwards or backwards according to the dictates of the selected stroke.

England wicket-keeper Godfrey Evans was quoted in his biography written by Christopher Sanford as follows:

BRADMAN REVISITED

To Evans he was absolutely concentrated and determined with a back-lift away and out towards point which would come down in a circle finishing straight to the line of the ball. Neither elegant nor spectacular - but a genius.

Evans was an ideal person to pass such a judgement. Apart from being one of England's greatest wicket-keepers, he also kept wicket to Bradman during two entire series.

Nonetheless, there is some misunderstanding on how wide Bradman's batting movement was. Earlier in my research I had the good fortune to meet Jack Potter, former inaugural head coach to the Australian cricket academy, who showed great interest in my project (and has continued to do so). I gave him a copy of my notes as they were at the time, and, after his return to Australia, I was flattered to hear that he took the trouble to send them to Sir Don Bradman. I am happy to quote Sir Donald's reply in full, while pointing out that he always refuted suggestions made to him in later life that he was the greatest batsman of all and when asked to explain his statistical superiority simply replied this was for others to worry about:

I read Tony's words with interest and some embarrassment because I lay no claims to the expertise with which he credits me.

In general I think many coaches stifle the natural abilities of young players by rigidly insisting that they do not move until the ball is delivered and that they adhere to a perpendicular bat with left hand control. Movie strips of me batting indicate that I started my backlift before the ball was delivered and that the bottom of my bat was approximately level with the tops of the stumps at the instant of delivery.

But let me hasten to say my backlift was rather towards 2nd slip - not point as some suggest.

The perpendicular bat theory virtually eliminates pull shots (which can only be played with a cross bat) and square cuts (except by angling the blade which, in turn, is a recipe for giving catches in the slips).

If Tony has not got a copy of my book 'The Art of Cricket' he should get one because my movements are clearly defined in movie strips.

This appears to contradict Godfrey Evans (and others) but is really a matter of perception. The important issue, of when he started his movement, is confirmed. Movements happen almost in the blink of an eye and for shots such as the hook or the square cut, no doubt they would 'appear' circular. They did to Evans!

In other words, the selected shot would alter the appearance of the bat's movement. What is important is that it was the 'rotary' action which provided the smoothness, and it was this motion of the hands, wrists, arms, shoulders and bat which, from his closed-face stance, allowed him the scope to score all around the wicket with such freedom.

Having studied the Bradman method on newsreel footage and experimented with it at length, former

BRADMAN REVISITED

Australian captain, and one of the great batsmen of the post Bradman era, Greg Chappell, had a very interesting observation on early movement:

Basically Bradman didn't lift the bat at all - he levered it up. He just pushed down with the top hand and used the thumb and forefinger of his bottom hand as a fulcrum. There was no lifting as such; it was a pure lever action. The result was that the bat virtually weighed nothing because it was pointing straight up.

The need for a backlift is a fallacy. You don't need a backlift. All you need to do is get the bat into a neutral position so you can move quickly to play the ball, both forwards and back.

Once he'd levered the bat up Bradman's hands were in the middle of his body and his balance was perfect. Bradman was just so loose because he levered the bat up it was almost weightless, so it didn't take much effort to hold it.

From Bradman's normal stance and grip this viewpoint perhaps tends to support Godfrey Evans. The passage of his bat would start somewhere around 3rd or 4th slip to gully before continuing its rotary movement. But in any event, C.B. Fry would fully approve of Chappell's observations on balance and the need to be free to react.

It brings us back to Bradman's beginnings and his boyhood game with golf ball and stump. The same rotary action used to control that fast-moving golf ball was the essence of Bradman's movement throughout his career.

Remembering the good record Alec Bedser had at bowling to Bradman towards the end of his career, I sought his advice on backlift, and was most gratified to receive a letter from Sir Alec which contained the following:

Your remarks regarding the picking up of the bat by Bradman. From my experience and observations all great batsmen picked the bat up in the direction of at least the second slip. Jack Hobbs, Hutton, Compton, May, Morris, Harvey, in fact all I bowled to. To me that is the only way to acquire flow of the bat.

Geoffrey Boycott has similar views:

If your stance is correct it is a natural movement to pick up your bat in the direction of slips. Then at the top of the backlift loop the bat and bring it down over the line of the stumps.

On another occasion Boycott went further than this:

Many teachers suggest you take the bat back directly over the middle stump. I feel the best players have never done this. It is simply not a natural movement and it will let you down under pressure.

BRADMAN REVISITED

It appears there is a consensus view on batting movement. Despite this, the MCC have produced a coaching video to go with the official coaching book 'Masterclass', which clearly shows a group of youngsters being supervised in the pendulum movement of the bat. Like robots these youngsters are grouped together under the watchful eyes of the coach with their bats suspended in the air straight back in the direction of where their wickets would be. Geoffrey Boycott openly contradicts this form of early movement in the coaching book 'Masterclass' - as previously quoted.

So the video shows one thing, and Boycott (and apparently all great batsmen) believes differently. It appears the MCC have some explaining to do. Up and down the country youngsters are being taught slavishly to take their bats straight back. The indications are that they are being given a handicap from the very beginning.

Early on in my studies I realised that before I became too involved in theory, comparing different batting methods, and in particular my perception of Don Bradman, I would have to begin at the beginning to see if I could master it myself.

Fortunately I was able to use the excellent facilities of my local club and, armed with a light plastic 'Kwik' cricket bat and a tennis ball, I began hitting the rebounding ball against the wall (granted, a much easier task than Bradman's golf ball and stump game, but I consoled myself that I was at the end of my career and not the beginning!).

BRADMAN'S SECRET

Initially, to my disappointment, I found I was losing control of the ball after 10 - 12 hits. It wasn't until I remembered the continual motion of Bradman's bat that things changed. Instead of hitting the ball and returning the bat ready for the next hit I began carrying the bat right through the ball and round in a smooth loop using the natural rotation of the shoulders, thereby maintaining continuous movement in order to keep the ball in play. Footwork followed automatically.

Within a short space of time practising in this manner I found the results were very satisfying. I could keep the ball in play for long periods with little apparent strain either mental or physical. The action itself allows concentration and watching the ball to become automatic. Feet move instinctively to the line of the ball as it rebounds from the wall whilst the bat controls the ball through the instinctive adjustments of the wrists, hands and fingers in order to make the next hit manageable.

Anybody who practises hitting a ball against a wall in this manner will begin to sense the feel and co-ordination of Bradman's batting motion.

So far so good, but understanding and proving to myself the early development stages of Bradman's batsmanship as a youngster was one thing. I had to try to move from the 'laboratory experimental' stage to actuality. This meant net practice and proper cricket. Although my serious cricketing days were behind me I had never actually stopped playing - albeit at a lower level and not as regularly. So, as a start, I took my new--found batting style to the nets.

BRADMAN REVISITED

After playing a good standard of club cricket for nearly 45 years using the 'orthodox' method, I found the adjustment to this new grip, stance and backlift very difficult. I did not feel right and found timing was also a problem. I found myself consciously thinking of technique as each ball came down. So much so that I forgot the crucially necessary early movement. I had not been reacting until the ball was actually in flight. Once I began moving the bat prior to delivery of the ball, I found a dramatic improvement. Batting was not just different, with practice it suddenly became a thrilling new experience. As long as the speed of the bowling on the indoor surface was within my capacity, the sight of the ball did, in Bradman's words, trigger a corresponding reaction. Never before in my cricketing experience had I timed the ball so consistently well, nor hit it so fast all around the wicket and with so little mental and physical effort.

When Bradman's aggressive intent and determination is considered, together with the additional freedom and scope of his method, it becomes possible to come to terms with his remarkable record.

After further practice, I had the satisfaction of employing my 'new style' in proper cricket matches - admittedly at a modest level. My conclusion is that I will always regret not playing in this manner throughout my career. I felt at home, in command and knew that when I lost my wicket, it had less to do with style and more to do with advancing years. It is frustrating to reflect that as a schoolboy cricketer, I had started this way and been transformed by a well-meaning, but mistaken coach.

BRADMAN'S SECRET

To complete the sequence of a Bradman picture, the bowler arrives at the wicket and starts his bowling action. Prior to the ball's release, Bradman's closed face bat begins its rotary movement towards the area of the slips at the same time he is lifted on to the balls of both feet. He is now in the perfect position of balance for shot selection - forward or backward.

That Bradman performed this same early batting movement for every ball up to shot selection meant his timing and motion became second nature. The state of mind required for this to happen has recently been brought to light in an interesting manner.

When previewing the autobiography of Michael Atherton, The Times made a special feature of his famous 10-hour match-saving innings of 185 not out, played at the Wanderers, Johannesburg, in 1995.

Atherton introduces the term 'zone' to describe the type of concentration essential to this performance, which he describes in the following manner:

For the only time in my career I was in the 'zone'. I was in an almost trance-like state. Everything happened dreamily, in slow motion, although I was still alert and picking up the cues around me. The 'zone' was a state of both inertia and intense concentration and I knew that I was in total control and they couldn't get me out.

I couldn't begin to explain how to replicate it. I don't think I ever completely experienced it again. The 'zone' to me was a feeling of absolute control.

BRADMAN REVISITED

It is clear from this description that what Atherton calls the 'zone' is a form of automatic pilot. Earlier in this narrative I have quoted C.B. Fry describing this ideal - when batting becomes "an unconscious, subconscious habit". This is apparently what happened to Atherton on this occasion but, by his own admission, it happened only once in a long career. This is where Bradman was so different. Having grown accustomed to the conditions and played himself in, his training and method appears to have allowed him to enter this 'zone' almost as a matter of course. The state of the game had little effect. Bradman's 'zone' ensured he was never dismissed during the nineties in a Test innings, while of 669 innings in all cricket 211 were centuries, of which 41 were double centuries, eight trebles and one quadruple.

I believe the various lessons used over the years to explain Bradman's superiority miss this essential point. Quite simply what I have described as a 'rotary action' - developed from his boyhood game - was the basis whereby Bradman entered the 'zone' more easily than any other player before or since.

It was his method that was the bedrock of his success, not any other supposed advantages, be they physical or mental. Any of the latter could only develop as a result of this method. By Bradman's own admission, without it he could not have achieved his success.

3.

FOOTWORK AND BALANCE

The importance of footwork and balance to quality batsmanship has long been understood and cannot be overstated. Balance is, of course, mainly dependent on footwork. C. B. Fry had this to say:

It may seem absurd to say that what he does or leaves undone with his feet makes much more difference to a batsman than what he does or leaves undone with his hands, for it is by means of his footwork, and by this means alone, that he can bring his bat into effective relation with the ball. It is only by appropriate movement of one foot or the other - or of first one and then the other - that the various well-known strokes are possible.

It matters how you move your feet after the ball has left the face of the bat as well as how you move them before. For with the feet rigidly fixed not only is it impossible to begin the stroke correctly, but it is impossible to finish the stroke freely. The fixity of the feet pins the shoulders and thus reduces the power of following through to practically nil.

In his treatise on batting written early in the 20th century, and to which I have frequently referred, Fry seems to have given a preview of some of Bradman's greatest strengths.

BRADMAN REVISITED

When first experimenting for myself with Bradman's grip, stance and early backlift at the nets, I was more readily able to understand the liberating effect in regard to the movement of the feet and easy sense of balance.

The type of footwork induced by the Bradman style of batting is different because the bat is already moving away (not immediately behind) from the body, taking the balance forward onto the toes of each foot even before the actual stroke has been selected. The feet are thus freer to react quickly and instinctively as required to play the selected stroke.

I liken this process to that of the fielder who is walking in very quickly as the bowler approaches the crease. As soon as the ball is struck, his feet will move immediately in any direction to field it. Such fieldsmen also tend to adopt an alert, semi-crouching position similar to Bradman as he prepared to play his shots.

The balance obtained by the Bradman style compares favourably to that obtained by the more orthodox approach where the weight is not so evenly distributed. Greg Chappell does not mince his words on the subject: "The reason he's the best player ever is that he was the best balanced player ever." Chappell also wrote:

Bradman was a bit like a boxer who carries his hands low, like Muhammed Ali. He was on the balls of his feet light as a feather. He never took the bat outside the perimeter of his feet.

If you try to lift the bat straight back, all of a sudden you're using a lot of muscles in your hands, forearms, upper arms, chest - and once you engage those muscles, it requires effort from your legs to keep you balanced.

In Chappell's view this was a big advantage of the Bradman method. The weight of the bat was over his feet rather than projected behind him beyond his centre of gravity. This avoided the shift in weight to the back foot produced by a traditional backlift.

Chappell's research suggests that regardless of what the textbooks say, most good players over the years have tended towards the Bradman pick-up, although not perhaps quite as he did. This begs the question, why do the coaching manuals totally exclude this style? Bradman's footwork and balance would appear to provide him with an immediate and obvious advantage.

From this position, to play off the back foot the weight initially transfers more easily to the front foot, so allowing the bat and the back foot to move together in one co-ordinated movement when seeking the correct position to play the ball.

Similarly for front foot strokes, the weight more easily transfers to the back foot, so enabling the front foot and bat to seek the ideal hitting position.

As Neville Cardus put it: "Apparently he is free to play off any foot".

It was Bradman's balance which gave him this facility. He was able to quickly shift his weight to either foot so giving him a firm base for his stroke. His rotary movement and grip allowed flexibility for his hands to control the precision placement for which he was famous.

BRADMAN REVISITED

Commentators regularly draw attention to batsmen who lack footwork, particularly when most vulnerable early in their innings.

In practice, combined with aggressive intent, a special feature of the timing and motion of the 'Rotary' style is that the feet are induced to move quickly and automatically to every ball faced.

While I was in the company of Jack Potter (Australian Cricket Academy), someone asked him how he thought Bradman would have handled Shane Warne. His response was immediate: "Bradman would not have let him pitch." Perhaps a bit of an exaggeration considering Warne's status in world cricket since he bowled his famous 'Gatting Ball', but I understood his thought process. The freeing of the feet allowed by Bradman's method would have given him a major advantage over most batsmen in getting quickly to the pitch of the ball in a controlled manner. Dealing with Warne from the 'orthodox' position has distinct disadvantages.

Dennis Compton's view would tend to support Jack Potter:

He had a marvellous gift of getting into position quicker than any batsman I have ever seen, played the ball very late and was never off balance, or stretching out of control.

Bradman's footwork and balance are therefore seen as fundamental reasons for his success. These are not dependent on any physical advantages as we have shown earlier. They are a product of early training and batting style, a style openly discouraged by most English coaches.

4.

STROKE PLAY

Through modern technology we are now able to see, on our TV screens, the reaction time allowed a batsman as the bowler releases the ball. In the case of a fast bowler it is just under half a second; for a slow bowler, twice as long.

It seems incredible that in this time frame a batsman has to assess both line and length, select the stroke to be played, and carry it through to completion. It therefore seems highly unlikely a batsman, particularly against quicker bowling, has not begun to react before the ball is in flight. Bradman had no doubts about this and his statement is so important it bears repeating again:

In theory one could make a case for standing still and not moving the bat until you see the ball in the air and know where it is pitching. In practice this doesn't happen and I am all in favour of the batsman starting to lift his bat and make a preliminary movement with his feet before the ball is actually delivered.

Many top batsmen have become renowned as either front foot or back foot players. It is how they feel most 'at home'. It is, however, unlikely that anyone learning to bat with a golf ball and stump, as did Bradman (or Hobbs who did something similar), would become a predominately forward player. It is more natural to move back in order to take advantage of the extra fraction of a second allowed to see and control the ball. It is, of course, the length of the ball which largely dictates movement - whether forward or backwards, but there is the 'area of uncertainty' which the bowler seeks to find on the wicket which has the batsman in two minds. With Bradman this could be less of a problem - he would react as his instinct, grip, stance and early movement naturally guided him - on to his back foot. Under normal circumstances Bradman went forward only when able to get close to the pitch of the ball. In 'The Art of Cricket' he had this to say:

History shows that the outstanding batsmen were mostly strong off the back foot. They could drive of course, but their initial protective movement was back rather than forward.

Ranji expressed himself very much in favour of back play and went on to say: "No forward stroke is absolutely safe unless the ball is smothered." By that I assume he meant it had to be played as a genuine half volley. No batsman can fail to get into difficulty if he persists in driving well away from his body.

Throughout his career Bradman was renowned more than most other great batsmen for keeping the ball on the ground. His statement helps to clarify why this was so. If he couldn't confidently get close to the pitch of the ball, he played back particularly to the quicker bowlers. To the slower bowlers his balanced early position allowed him to make ground very quickly to drive or smother as required.

BRADMAN REVISITED

Sir Pelham Warner illustrates this clearly:

Bradman seldom played forward. He is either right back or feet out of his ground attacking the bowler. He is always attacking. The cut, both late and square, is his glory. I have never seen finer or safer cutting, for he is always on top of the ball.

The South African fast bowler A. J. Bell, who bowled against Bradman in seven matches in 1931 without getting his wicket, supports this:

Most people in South Africa seem to be under the impression that Bradman is a great forward player. This is quite erroneous. He is the finest back foot player any of us have ever seen.

The evocative pen-pictures of great players drawn by Neville Cardus over much of the 20th century have entertained millions of cricket lovers the world over. I am delighted to repeat an earlier quote of his on this subject:

He scored a hundred in an hour with restraint. Now and again, true, he reached forward in a way not common for Bradman, who is a back foot player if ever there was one.

That Bradman was primarily a back foot player is clearly established by these, and many other writings. But this does not imply a weakness playing forward. Chart plans produced to illustrate some of his greatest innings show he appeared to score runs to all parts of the ground. There was no recognised cricket stroke which was not in his repertoire off either front or back foot. But all writers on Bradman are clear about one point - he dictated to the bowlers. It was his batting style that permitted this. The distribution of weight, and therefore balance, obtained by the pendulum style of batting occupies fractions of a second longer to adjust. The scientific research carried out at Liverpool's John Moores University also found that Bradman's technique allowed the player time to delay shot selection.

Of all the quotations used about Bradman, probably the most significant is the one in which Jim Laker says that Bradman is the only batsman he ever bowled to who gave him an inferiority complex. Once established at the wicket, it was Bradman who dictated the line and length of the bowler to a degree rarely seen by other great batsmen.

It is well to compare the balanced position and movement of Bradman's method with the orthodox method - whereby the batsman stands with an open-faced bat, sometimes held behind the rear toes and sometimes held horizontally backwards.

When commencing the back-lift from this position, weight, including that of the arms and bat, transfers instinctively to the back foot. C.B. Fry has, as usual, a point to make:

The smallest, almost imperceptible, swaying of the upper part of the body transfers weight from one foot to the other.

BRADMAN REVISITED

The orthodox movement has an uneven weight distribution and leaves two options when playing back:

1. Transfer the weight back to the front foot to release the rear foot in order to play the stroke, so wasting precious time.
2. Simply shift the weighted back foot in the hope of getting in line and the correct position to play the stroke. This movement lacks balance and co-ordination and induces poor footwork.

According to research by Australian cricket coach John Harmer (into the maximising effect of body movement), 80% of all dismissals are caused by poor footwork. This is summed up perfectly by Wilfred Rhodes:

The art of bowling is to get the batsman's feet in the wrong place.

It was obvious from Bradman's grip, stance and early movement that his stroke play would differ from those with a more 'orthodox' style. The natural rotation of his movements meant that his bat and body would be brought close together with his head close to the line of the ball. When making attacking strokes the bat would continue its motion 'through' the ball, his flexible grip ensuring the ball was played to ground. The closing motion of Bradman's bat meant he was less likely to be caught at the wicket, while the continuing momentum of the follow through would lead naturally into the taking of a run.

This is in contrast to the pendulum style of a straight backlift whereby the bat tends to 'follow' the ball rather than close on it. With this sideways movement there is also a tendency for a batsman to reach for the ball which is beyond his normal control.

Whatever style a batsman adopts, orthodox or otherwise, some shots come easier than others. In Bradman's case he accepted that his style made it more difficult for him to score in the arc between mid-off and point. He did not, however, consider this sufficient a reason to alter his approach. He considered the advantages more than compensated for any inconveniences. In any case, a study of any of Bradman's big innings shows that he scored plenty of runs in his 'difficult' area!

Wristwork

While the importance of wristwork towards the art of batting has long been acknowledged, little has been written about it.

However, a summary of Bradman's strokeplay would not be complete without mentioning the special use of his wrists, hands and fingers. After all, despite the importance of head and feet it is the grip and feel of these upon the bat which offers a player the fine-tuning of ultimate control.

Anyone copying or using a version of Bradman's boyhood game will quickly come to understand how Bradman's mature batting method gave him an instant advantage over orthodox players who are relatively restricted when adopting the 'cock-wristed' pendulum style.

By contrast the synchronised body motion emanating from Bradman's closed faced stance enabled his wrists to rotate in unison with complete flexibility as if on ball-bearings within a socket. This range of movement leading to control facilitated the playing of strokes to all corners of the field.

At one and the same time the rotary wrist action would offer power of shot while allowing hands and fingers the touch to provide the precision placement for which Bradman was famous. An added bonus to this style being the ability to adjust and play late as the wrists automatically turn on the ball and hit it to ground.

This manner of using hands and wrists cannot be divorced from the batting method which arose from Bradman's boyhood game and cannot therefore be taught as an entity by itself. By this I mean that such wristwork cannot naturally come from the orthodox stance and pendulum motion of the bat.

Together with a light bat, the use of the wrists, hands and fingers is a key element of Bradman's batting and is fundamental to any understanding of how he constantly amazed players and spectators alike with his ability to find gaps in the field.

Following eight years of study, if asked to highlight any one aspect of Bradman's batting which assisted his free-scoring capabilities it would be that, as an integral part of the rotary method, his wrist play offered a scope and versatility of stroke not available to the orthodox batsman.

5.

PHYSICAL AND MENTAL ASPECTS

In previous chapters we have shown how contemporary explanations for Bradman's unique success as a batsman tended to concentrate on physical and mental aspects at the expense of technique. An "abnormally quick reaction"; "icily concentrated mind"; "eyes, feet and wrists that see and work just a fraction quicker than the ordinary great players" (E.W. Swanton); "Gets into position quicker than any batsman I have ever seen" (Dennis Compton); "Confidence supreme" (Wilfred Rhodes). Such descriptions of his strokes as there are describe their appearance rather than how he produced them.

To perform as he did, Bradman had to be extremely fit, and unquestionably, he took great care to maintain his fitness. It is, however, very doubtful if any physical attributes marked him apart from his leading contemporaries. We have already demonstrated that the contrary is more likely.

A close look at Bradman's mental make-up points to a different conclusion. It was here that some of his attributes marked him out to be amongst a very select band indeed. Principal amongst some of these virtues are an analytical brain, great patience and great determination. One does not have to be a qualified psychiatrist to reach this conclusion, the briefest study of his life makes them apparent.

Apart from being one of cricket's 'greats', Bradman was also an excellent golfer, a good tennis player and a very good pianist. With regard to the latter, he could apparently play well 'by ear' as well as from music; a skill requiring many hours of practice. It also shows the ability to improvise - which was very much a part of his attacking stroke play! To be proficient at any one of these arts would be enough for most of us who are performing for pleasure but who still have to make a living in the workplace.

It is obvious that for Bradman there were no half measures. If he took an interest in something he had to become good at it and not just 'play around'.

Lovers of cricket are fortunate that it was with this sport that Bradman seemed to find the ultimate challenge.

It is worth re-emphasising that Bradman only developed his batting skills after initially, at play, developing all the mental and physical skills necessary for him to become the finished article. Like Jack Hobbs he was never coached. At the very beginning of his career he found these skills, no doubt with some adaptation, quite sufficient for him to attain outstanding success at school and in his short career with his club, Bowral.

It was his arrival at the scene of State cricket, fresh from the country, where his mental strengths first began to show themselves. His grip and stance immediately marked him as different to other budding stars of his era. He noticed for himself he was a 'one-off', so very soon experimented at net practice with the more orthodox approach. He was to write:

CAPTION 1 CAPTION 2

OFF DRIVE

STRAIGHT DRIVE

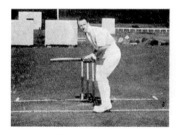 

ON DRIVE

These sequence pictures of Bradman demonstrating some of his attacking strokes are from the early 1930s when he was in his prime. They should be viewed laterally across the pages and overleaf.

CAPTION 1: Shows Bradman's initial response before shot selection. His balanced style is uncommitted with bat in motion.

CAPTION 2: Decision time. Bradman's bat continues its loop as he prepares to drive off the front foot.

CAPTION 3 CAPTION 4

OFF DRIVE

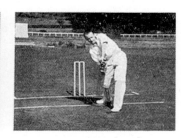

STRAIGHT DRIVE

ON DRIVE

CAPTION 3: By this time Bradman's foot has sought and found the hitting position as the flexible flow of his bat continues its 'rotary' motion. Even at this late stage final adjustments can be made.

CAPTION 4: Point of contact. Bradman uncoils as he drives with the full face of the bat.

CAPTION 5	CAPTION 6

OFF DRIVE

STRAIGHT DRIVE

ON DRIVE

CAPTION 5: Bradman's stroke is now fully committed as he hits through the line of the ball.

CAPTION 6: The automatic continuation of Bradman's wristwork becomes more apparent as the ball is played to ground.

CAPTION 7

OFF DRIVE

STRAIGHT DRIVE

ON DRIVE

CAPTION 7

Completion. Although driving with full power Bradman remains balanced with head still.
In the sequence of pictures featuring the on drive the closeness of Bradman's head to the line of the ball, together with its stillness up to the point of contact, has been well highlighted by the camera against the background sightscreen.

| **CAPTION 1** | **CAPTION 2** |

HOOK

PULL

JUMPING OUT TO DRIVE

Although there are similarities between the 'pull' and the 'hook' strokes as illustrated, the 'pull' is forward of square in the area of mid-wicket, whilst the 'hook' is much finer, backward of square. In Bradman's case this would depend upon the height at which the ball is played. In making these shots Bradman has moved inside the line of the ball, pivoting on his anchor leg outside off stump whilst still retaining his balance.

CAPTION 3   CAPTION 4

HOOK

PULL

JUMPING OUT TO DRIVE

All the pictures in all these sequences give a clear indication
of the importance played by Bradman himself on the
complete stroke as a whole. This incorporates the early 'pick-
up' of the bat, use of wrists, and complete follow through in
one continuous motion. It is also imperative to remember that
it is this initial outward movement of the bat which creates
the smooth flow.

CAPTION 5 **CAPTION 6**

 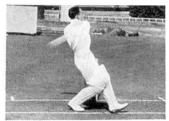

HOOK

PULL

JUMPING OUT TO DRIVE

The bottom series of pictures show Bradman 'jumping' far down the wicket to drive. His easy balance style allowed him to do this quickly. Although generally accepted as a back foot player, it was this ability which highlighted the bowler's dilemma when attempting to stem the flow of runs.
When asked the question as to how Bradman would have coped with Shane Warne, Jack Potter, inaugural head coach of the Australian Cricket Academy, replied that Bradman would not have let him pitch the ball!

CAPTION 7

HOOK

PULL

The final picture of Bradman jumping out to drive is not, unlike with the hook and pull, the completed shot. The completed shot is illustrated in the final photo section.

JUMPING OUT TO DRIVE

BRADMAN'S SECRET

I experimented, worked out the pros and cons and eventually decided not to change my natural grip.

Although Bradman was a teenager at this time, he showed an extraordinary self-belief and strength of character to virtually say to all the cricket establishment "Thank you very much, I've tried your method but believe that mine is best for me." Nothing big-headed or arrogant, but a simple statement of fact. This was to be typical of the Bradman that the cricket world would get to know. The important point being, he listened, reasoned it out, experimented and then backed his own judgement.

He brought this same analytical approach to back-lift, deciding, as we have seen, that the 'straight back-lift', or pendulum style, might be better for defence, but that it restricted attacking shots. He thought about it, tried it - and rejected it. It appears he accepted that he was different, understood the technical differences and simply carried on in the simple belief that his method was best for him.

Which brings us to his mental approach to scoring runs. In one of his rare television interviews, he quietly maintained his belief that if possible he should score off every ball! Not for him the negative thought of defending his wicket. To him, the best way of defending his wicket was to score runs. It was that simple - he went to the wicket with aggressive intent - a trait openly encouraged in their teams by modern day Australian captains Mark Taylor and Steve Waugh.

All of this of course is of little use if you have not got the basic ability. Bradman makes no secret of his success.

BRADMAN REVISITED

Practice, practice and more practice. To learn to play the piano takes hours of rehearsing scales until they become easy. What Bradman did with his piano he also did with his batting. Just as playing the piano eventually becomes a habit - so does scoring runs. There is no substitute for dedication and hard work, a point Bradman makes time and again.

This belief in his own 'star', based on confidence in the very personal style of batting he had evolved, together with endless practice, produced the Don Bradman whom the cricketing world held in awe. The pen-picture passed down to us by many writers of a rather small man walking out to the wicket and taking guard with half a smile on his face, completes the picture of a man at ease with himself and confident that he will prevail.

Former MCC President H.S. Altham says it best in a quotation much appreciated by the Don himself:

In the many pictures that I have stored in my mind from the burnt-out junes of 40 years, there is none more dramatic and compelling than that of Bradman's small, serenely moving figure in big peaked green cap coming out of the pavilion shadows into the sunshine, with the concentration, ardour and apprehension of surrounding thousands centred upon him and the destiny of a Test match in his hands.

6.

CRICKET EQUIPMENT

With the exception of his bat a cricketer's main equipment is concerned with self-protection. Most advice concerning gloves, pads, boxes and footwear is common sense, but the subject of cricket bats needs much closer scrutiny.

In the official MCC coaching book 'Masterclass', it says:

A young player needs a bat that is easy in the pick-up, not too heavy, with a good drive, and one with which he feels comfortable. Advice should be sought from a coach rather than a parent buying a bat in a shop that does not specialise in bats. The coach will also advise about the oiling of the bat - never on the splice and not excessively.

This is good advice - but not very easy to follow. For example, in 1947 Dennis Compton hit 18 centuries and scored 3,816 runs with a bat weighing 2 lbs. 2 ozs. Such bats are no longer generally available to the public. Heavier bats are now 'fashionable' - made so by physically powerful men such as Ian Botham and Clive Lloyd. Botham used a bat weighing about 3½ lbs. The youth of any generation tend to emulate their heroes and this appears to have resulted in an absence of bats on offer at the lighter end of the weight scale.

BRADMAN REVISITED

One of England's all-time great batsmen, Walter Hammond, had strong views on the subject and in his book, 'Cricketer's School', had this to say:

In general the chief danger is buying too heavy a bat. With two or three exceptions the finest batsmen, Bradman, McCabe, Harvey, Washbrook, Hobbs, Ranjitsinhji among them - have used lighter bats, which enabled them to get the maximum quickness from their wrists. In cricket's 'Golden Age' in the opening years of this century, it was customary to use a much lighter bat than is now the custom in County cricket; and in those days, both footwork and wrist work were infinitely quicker than they are in England today.

If you chose a bat that is a little too light for you no harm will be done; the only drawback may be that you will have to learn to hit a little harder to reach the boundary though even this is far more a matter of 'middling' the ball in the thick part of the bat. But if you chose too heavy a bat you will become slow; and in batting slowness is the most fatal of all faults.

Hammond wrote this almost half a century ago, what he would think of today's bats, which are even heavier, can only be imagined. But such basic requirements for good batsmanship, as quoted from his book, are for all time. If, as seems reasonable, balance and footwork - especially speed of movement - are adversely affected by heavy bats, this is obviously a subject that requires thorough investigation.

BRADMAN'S SECRET

There is no doubt Bradman agreed with Hammond's views as he spoke out in favour of lighter bats himself.

Throughout his career Bradman used short-handled bats weighing about 2 lbs. 5 ozs. We can safely conclude that his famed speed of reaction, both of bat and body, were partly dependent upon his equipment, of which his bat would be the most important item. It is the control he exercised over his light bat that encouraged his 'aggressive intentions' and the initiative and improvisation of his play.

During the course of this study, when watching batsmen, I have become increasingly aware of the direct relationship between the initial timing and motion of the bat with both good and bad footwork. In general terms, the more the batsman relies on 'orthodox technique' to the exclusion of judgement and co-ordination, the greater his problems. If Bradman and Hammond are correct, heavy bats will inhibit good footwork and encourage slower reaction.

The average size and weight of cricketers has increased since the Bradman/Hammond days, but the disadvantages of bigger and heavier bats have not had sufficient airing, and are not dealt with adequately in MCC's coaching manual. It is also possible that hand and finger injuries and heavy bats are not unconnected, as these bats with their 'fatter' handles require a stronger grip.

As part of these researches I tried, initially without success, to buy a light bat of the type used by Compton during his great year in 1947. Eventually, a local sports dealer and friend contacted former England wicket-keeper Bob Taylor, who, at that time, was working as a sports representative. To my delight, Bob had a 'Dukes' bat specially made for me - weighing 2 lbs. 2 ozs, the same as Compton's 'magic bat'. Too late to help me in my own career, I use it for demonstration purposes and net practice. It is a delight. But the disturbing question arises - are the bats currently available to budding young batsmen adequate to all needs?

Much more can be said on this subject but in these days of centralised coaching it is a subject worthy of comprehensive investigation. It should be noted that the only hit ever to clear the Lord's Pavilion was made in 1902 by Albert Trott (an Australian who played Test Match cricket for both Australia and England!) using a bat probably weighing 2 lbs, 2 ozs.

7.

CONCLUSION

Towards the end of my research, which has taken me close to eight years, Sir Donald Bradman died. The famous headline of yesteryear, "He's Out", took on a sad new meaning. Like cricket fans the world over I felt the sadness that comes with the knowledge that we will never know his like again, for I had begun to realise early on that Sir Donald was not simply a uniquely great batsman, but also a very remarkable human being.

When Ray Martin did his famous television interview with Sir Donald to commemorate his 87th birthday, it was difficult to know which to admire most - Bradman the great cricketer or Bradman the human being. It inspired me in my research and his recent passing made me more determined than ever to attempt to explain the legacy he has left to the cricket world.

Bradman developed a style of batting that was different to the accepted orthodoxy. Other great batsmen have been 'unorthodox', and some of them were similar - up to a point, but as far as my research has been able to reveal, nobody had exactly the same grip, stance and early movement as the Don. He truly was unique.

It was pure circumstance that, as a boy, Bradman developed his skills with one aim in mind; how to control a fast-moving golf ball with a cricket stump as it rebounded from a brick wall onto a concrete floor.

Control is the operative word, and by achieving this, he unknowingly incorporated all the natural skills required to become a top class batsman.

He had no preconceived ideas of technique, but the skills he developed in his 'solo' game enabled him to evolve a batting style which possessed a scope for scoring runs that has so far proved beyond the capabilities of 'accepted orthodoxy'. He did not possess any unusual physical advantages - of either eyesight or physical strength - that could explain his dominance. What he did have is an unshakeable belief that the batting style he had evolved was best - at least for him. He had tried the orthodox style and rejected it as it had, to quote him, "greater limitations in versatile stroke-making".

I hope that my analysis will open up a debate on the very nature of 'orthodoxy' in batting, and that, as a consequence, budding young cricketers will be allowed to develop their natural talents free from dogma. In the introduction to his book 'How to Play Cricket', Bradman wrote:

I do hope the value of my experience will be within the reach of everybody.

It is time for cricket to respect this wish as a lasting tribute to the memory of the world's most successful batsman.

PART THREE

Reflections and Observations

BRADMAN REVISITED

IF THE FIRST TWO SECTIONS were mainly concerned with highlighting the Bradman years and explaining his unique pre-eminence and style, this final section will be concerning his legacy.

The Don Bradman era, lasting from 1928 to 1948 as a player, is now long past, as are many of the great players and writers whose observations have helped me to give reason and understanding to his success. However, the beauty is that while names change, the fundamentals of hitting and controlling a cricket ball remain for all time.

This book will have been largely a waste of my time if, at its conclusion, it is put aside as merely a half-decent read or an interesting theory. The whole purpose has been to promote a re-think of some of cricket's long held attitudes and tenets. Sacred cows, if you like. Upon this and nothing else the success of this venture stands or falls.

This section is therefore concerned with what can be learned; perhaps a development of themes touched upon earlier in the narrative, and also a glimpse into what might be.

1.

WILL THERE BE
ANOTHER BRADMAN?

Lovers of cricket are fascinated by this question and love to speculate. Most are content to fall back on the 'one-off genius' approach, and, by most critical judgement, as a batsman he was certainly a genius.

After Bradman's death on 25th February 2001, David Frith, former founding editor of Wisden Cricket Monthly, headed his moving tribute with the famous caption; 'He's Out!' The concluding paragraph of his article reads:

> *Time, they say, takes care of everything. Time has done what some of the finest bowlers of successive generations failed to do; it has removed D.G. Bradman from the batting crease. In his lifetime nobody matched his dominance or his staggering figures. And while it may be foolhardy to suppose anything is forever in cricket, it seems certain nobody ever will. Don Bradman was not one in a million. He was much rarer than that.*

David Frith is an acknowledged authority on cricket and the author of many books on the subject. This quote from his tribute makes clear his view on the possibility of our seeing another Bradman. It is a view shared by most cricket lovers.

BRADMAN REVISITED

Perhaps the question we should be asking ourselves is; is it reasonable, or desirable, for the game of cricket to accept, for all time and without question, the batting superiority of an uncoached Australian country boy?

Bradman himself had no doubts that his style of batting offered him greater scope where it mattered most - scoring runs. He made this point time and again, and I have quoted him freely. For him, 'perceived orthodoxy' had its limitations. This clearly suggests that a complete understanding of his style could well benefit the teaching of batsmanship the world over.

This has been the sole purpose of this research - to broaden thinking and to reduce dogma. It is not, I hasten to add, to replace one dogma with another. What Bradman found natural, comfortable and therefore effective, will not suit everyone. But to have his style and method not only untested, but also misunderstood and dismissed is, I believe, a fundamental mistake.

In more than 100 years of Anglo-Australian Test cricket, the greatest batsmen have come and gone with an average score of between 50 and 60. This law now applies to all Test-playing countries of all races and nationalities. The vast majority of these batsmen, but not all, have been coached in the methods of 'perceived orthodoxy' at some stage and to varying degrees. Bradman, un-coached and refusing to accept the tenets of this 'perceived orthodoxy', averaged close enough to 100. If his style, which is basically 'sound', though 'unorthodox', could be incorporated alongside more traditional methods of coaching, it would be fascinating to see if future batsmen could begin to narrow the huge performance gap

REFLECTIONS AND OBSERVATIONS

Bradman had established. Under the current system in England, this does not appear to be even a possibility.

However, irrespective of coaching methods, whether any batsman will ever actually match Bradman's feats remains a remote possibility and David Frith's comment about Bradman being "much rarer than one in a million" is fair enough.

Nevertheless, I see the very question, 'Will there be another Bradman?' as being a major obstacle towards an understanding of his batsmanship.

Those seeking the answer solely through the eyes of 'orthodoxy' have found Bradman's run-scoring impossible to take in and comprehend, so leading to a general acceptance of the 'one-off genius' syndrome and therefore a subsequent lack of will to query his methods.

Such acceptance from the orthodox perspective is understandable until one considers Bradman's stated view that even he could not have achieved such records had he batted in orthodox fashion.

It is not as if Bradman was better than other people at doing the same thing. His 'rotary' style was clearly different, so surely worthy of comprehensive study instead of the negative response which has prevailed to date.

2.

NATURAL BATTING, TECHNICAL BATTING

The investigations I have made have left me with the overriding impression that there are two different categories of batsmen - natural and technical.

To illustrate the meaning of this the following is taken from Don Bradman's 1935 instruction booklet, 'How to Play Cricket':

When a very small boy, cricket was to me the most wonderful game in the world (and, of course, it still is). Unfortunately however, being some distance from the Metropolis, I was unable to witness any first class cricketers in action. Actually, with the exception of a small portion of one Test match, I saw no first class cricket whatever until I was engaged in playing for New South Wales myself. Neither did I have the opportunity of reading any books on cricket by world famous players. Consequently, my entire cricketing experience has been a practical one.

In later years this booklet was adapted into video form with dialogue from Don Bradman himself. It is fascinating to hear Bradman not only describe the

REFLECTIONS AND OBSERVATIONS

physical playing of his strokes, but simultaneously describe the feel of the whole process using the following explanations:

1. Body poised for action as brain assesses direction and length of the ball.
2. Full balance and control.
3. Backlift still flexible.
4. Compact hitting position.
5. Body co-ordinated and unwound into the drive.
6. Watch and control the ball and hit through the stroke with a full follow through (ball not stabbed).
7. Swing body into line.
8. Feel everything moving along smoothly.
9. Rolling the blade over the ball.
10. Balance of stroke co-ordinated.

It is clear from his video that to Bradman, batting was an experience whereby the execution of a stroke was the end product in a sequence of smooth movements designed to give balance and co-ordination.

In similar fashion, Jack Hobbs, when summing up his youthful development with tennis ball and stump (so strangely reminiscent of Bradman) had this to say:

The straight stump helped me to sense the importance of the straight bat. Perhaps I tried to over flourish, but I learned to appreciate the grace, beauty, swing and rhythm of stroke play and, above all, balance.

BRADMAN REVISITED

As natural batsmen, both Bradman and Hobbs tend not to express their play solely in terms of technique, rather they stress the instinctive human rhythms and balance which allowed them the control and flexibility to shape the line and length of the ball to their benefit.

C.B. Fry was well aware of the relative importance of the more natural aspects of batting when writing:

There is probably a greater difference between good batsmen in the simple matter of how much they look at the ball, than in what amount of manual skill they possess.

This is an echo of Bradman's oft repeated "watch the ball and concentrate", as being the first pre-requisite leading to good judgement and therefore batting skill.

Fry goes on to say:

But the power of watching the ball completely is not in the majority of players a natural faculty; it needs to be cultivated and made an unconscious and subconscious habit. While the visual concentration remains a conscious effort it is not only liable to break down but is very tiring.

Perhaps by their similar development as boys, Bradman and Hobbs were able to naturally develop this habit of focussed concentration. In Bradman's case it would help to explain the consistent playing of long innings with an apparent lack of fatigue. What is certain is that both of these great batsmen learned to bat the natural way without recourse to formalised coaching in technique.

Due to greater formalisation and centralisation of coaching, batting has become far more technical, and this tends to produce batsmen who make a more cerebral type of judgement. Young players' heads are now filled with technical matter and their responses, having assessed line, length, speed and flight of a ball, tend to be drilled regulation strokes in a two-part mental and physical process which lacks the smooth co-ordination of the natural player.

As Fry says, the conscious effort of this type of concentration is not only liable to break down, but is very tiring. Perhaps here is an important part of the explanation to the age-old question, 'Why do set batsmen get themselves out?'

In Bradman's words, one must not be a slave to technique and should not have to be conscious of batting movements. They should be natural and involuntary.

In the same way there is a strong case for suggesting that an over-emphasis on technique is a handicap to bowlers attaining the loose co-ordinated body action so necessary in producing controlled natural swing. Perhaps this accounts for today's dearth in the swing bowling art.

Such emphasis may also go some way to explaining an apparent increase in injuries to bowlers, who are perhaps encouraged rather more to technical instruction than to using their natural rhythm and co-ordination as a means to sustaining control.

Coaching is no easy task, but sometimes I have the feeling instruction can be inclined more to the ideas of the coach than the need of the player concerned to express himself.

It is natural that Sachin Tendulkar, rated by many as the greatest batsman of the modern era, should be the subject of much media attention.

As well as extolling his many virtues, the inevitable comparisons have been made with Bradman, some commentators even going so far as to suggest parity between the two.

To support this view, references have been made to a famous 87th birthday television interview given by Bradman for Australian television and hosted by Ray Martin.

During the interview Bradman related that one day as his wife was watching Tendulkar bat on television, she called him from another room to say that Tendulkar reminded her of him as he once was.

Joining her, Bradman agreed and finished by saying, "All seemed to gel as far as I was concerned. That was how I felt." Importantly, the Don did not involve himself with any specific detail of this supposed similarity, such as grip, stance, movement and backlift.

Given the circumstances and the almost legendary close relationship between Jessie and himself, Bradman was hardly going to make it a point of disagreement. I rather think, therefore, too much is being made of this.

An article by Tim Adams in the Observer Sport Monthly, August 2002 edition, revealed not only similarities between Bradman and Tendulkar, but also fundamental differences.

REFLECTIONS AND OBSERVATIONS

In their own way both players developed exceptional hand-eye co-ordination, practiced assiduously and evolved not only distinctive styles but contrasting views on the fundamentals of batting.

Tendulkar, using a 3lb 2oz bat, suggests that, contrary to the manuals, great batting had little to do with the movement of the feet but is mostly about quickness of the hands and the stillness of the head.

Bradman, who used a 2lb 5 oz, bat states:

I doubt if one could truthfully say there is any single key to batsmanship, but footwork is certainly one of the keys to unlock the innermost secrets. It is to batting what a foundation is to a house. Without it there is no structure.

Tendulkar, with a heavy bat and an orthodox straighter backlift, is highly expert at powerful stroke play. On the other hand, Bradman, utilising a lighter bat and his 'rotary' style, relied upon quicker footwork to shape the line and length of the ball in order to keep the scoreboard moving.

Due to these differences, it is clear the construction and execution of the attacking strokes are therefore quite different. Nevertheless, both players agree, concentration and method need to be co-ordinated into subconscious habit. Echoes of C.B. Fry!

It is important to remind ourselves of Bradman's view of orthodoxy. On experimenting with it he found it "has greater limitations in versatile stroke-making". In other words, it was his own 'rotary' method that was responsible for his scoring feats.

BRADMAN REVISITED

Great batsman that Tendulkar undoubtedly is, his run scoring is in similar order to all other great batsmen past or present, Bradman excepted, in that he averages between 50 and 60 in Test Match cricket.

This leaves us to speculate whether Tendulkar, with his huge natural talent, could have closed the statistical gap with Bradman had he, as a young player, experimented with both batting methods, as Bradman did, and settled upon Bradman's.

The difference in Bradman's method cannot be over-emphasised. It was, in Jack Fingleton's words, "unlike any other batsman he ever saw."

N.B. The leading one-day batsmen in world cricket is the Australian Michael Bevan, with an average of approximately 55. This is far and away (almost 20%) higher than the next best, currently Tendulkar. Readers may like to compare Bevan's grip, stance and movement with descriptions of Bradman and note the similarities.

3.

OPINIONS AND DOGMA

Depending on whose opinions they are, sometimes these become dogma. The difficulty is whether opinions are fully explained and beyond misinterpretation. For example, speaking at the Test and County Cricket Board's seminar for 'first class county and N.C.A. coaches' early in 1980, Ted Dexter had this to say:

Neither an early pick-up nor an early foot movement has anything to recommend it. They can both be considered cardinal sins.

At first sight this seems clear enough, but what exactly did Dexter mean? What is early? If it means that neither bat nor feet should move before the ball leaves the bowler's hand, then this contradicts Bradman's statement in his book 'The Art of Cricket':

In theory you could make out a case for standing still and not moving the bat until you see the ball in the air and know where it is pitching.

In practice this doesn't happen and I am all in favour of the batsman starting to lift his bat and make a preliminary movement with his feet before the ball is actually delivered.

BRADMAN REVISITED

Bradman makes this point in explanation to a question frequently put to him as to why some batsmen seem to have more time than others do. Dexter's statement was made to a coaching seminar, and it would take a youngster of unusual character and independence to resist this advice by such an eminent authority.

Yet the more you study these statements the clearer it becomes that Bradman is right, and Dexter wrong, assuming that Dexter's statement is taken at face value. However, if all Dexter really meant was that too much exaggerated movement is bad, then most, including Bradman, might agree with him. In any event the words of Ted Dexter, one of England's greatest post-war batsmen, carry enormous weight. The coaching fraternity should be aware of his precise meaning, and, if applicable, understand that there is a difference of opinion between Dexter and Bradman on this fundamental point.

In similar vein there is an important difference of opinion regarding the position of the rear foot when shaping to play back-foot shots. Dexter has this to say:

It is the back foot position that matters so much. I have hardly seen a fine player whose back foot does not stay roughly parallel to the batting crease - and I emplore you, gentlemen, to make this a lynchpin of your instruction at all levels.

Bradman sees it differently and says:

Some coaches advocate that the toes shall remain parallel with the popping crease - others that they

136

*should point towards the bowler. I favour the happy
medium and think it best for the toes to be pointing
rather towards cover or mid-off.*

Both these great players were writing about making
strokes off the back foot. Dexter's view is inflexible;
Bradman's is not. The real point, however, is should
coaching be this dogmatic?

Sir Gary Sobers doesn't think so. In his book, 'Gary
Sobers' Way of Cricket', he writes:

*There is not one back foot defensive shot technique,
though many coaches and manuals dictate there is.*

We live in an era when coaching has become both
more formalised and centralised (MCC Masterclass). As
I have illustrated, the dangers of this are manifest. If
someone at the top gets an important point wrong (as I
also believe has happened with backlift), then many
thousands of youngsters are being misled by a video
intended to help develop their cricket prowess.

Just as dangerous is the compulsion to conform.
Individuality must never be discouraged. Dennis
Compton wrote:

*My style of play was soon to be discovered to be
unorthodox - though I might some day take the trouble
to enquire precisely what that word is supposed to
mean. Anyway whatever it means, I was not 'orthodox',
that fact was very obvious indeed and I suppose has
remained so for the whole of my life in cricket.*

137

BRADMAN REVISITED

This does not of course confine itself to batting. When Bradman was asked to name the greatest bowler he ever played against, his answer was - "Bill O'Reilly". Bradman went further than this when saying that his view was shared by all the first class batsmen he knew. He went on to say:

> *O'Reilly did not hold the ball in his fingers quite like the orthodox leg-spinner. It was held more towards the palm of the hand. He was advised by certain 'experts' to change his grip, but fortunately refused to be advised.*
>
> *This grip did not enable him to spin the ball very much but it did enable him to achieve phenomenal accuracy plus sufficient spin.*

The dangers of strict adherence to perceived orthodoxy are clear. Had Bradman, Compton, O'Reilly, Marshall, Jessop, Ranji and many others been taught as such from an early age, the world of cricket may well have been deprived of some of its all-time greats. This danger exists today more then ever before.

4.

BATTING PSYCHOLOGY

In previous chapters we touched on the early development of cricket in the 19th century, and also the theory of the 'straight bat' and its impact on the mental aspects of batting.

Whilst at Lord's as the guest of the 'Menzies Centre for Australian Studies' for their symposium commemorating the life of Sir Donald Bradman, I found time for a brief tour of the excellent Lord's Museum. One of the first items which came to my attention, in its dignified glass case, was a book entitled 'The Book of Games 1834', which happened to be open at a page which read:

One of the party who was out, bowled the ball from the distance of about 30 yards towards the wicket which it was the business of the batsman to defend. If he was fortunate enough to give it a good stroke he immediately set off to run as far as the line at 30 yards.

Some of the rules and terminology have changed but it was interesting to note that even in 1834 scoring runs came out very much secondary to the defence of the wicket (allowance must be made for the comparative uncertainty of the wickets in those days, which, by most accounts, were fairly rudimentary). While accepting that this subject can be viewed as a 'chicken and egg' situation, I believe that the emphasis has gradually become out of balance and that it is the duty of coaches to address this problem. Defence of the wicket, leading to the pendulum batting style, can have significant defensive overtones. At its worst it can lead to a sterile batting mentality, and is something we see all too frequently.

In his autobiography Cyril Washbrook has a chapter 'I find the silver lining'. It contains his thoughts about batting as he contemplates the restart of cricket after the Second World War. It states as follows:

Two factors contributed to any advance on my part. One was the practice received with Austin Matthews at Cambridge during the war. The other was the fact that, during those many hours in the R.A.F. when my thoughts had turned again and again to cricket, I had been struck by the realisation that nearly all the best batsmen I had seen or read about possessed one feature in common - they always sought to get on top of the bowler and not allow him to dictate the policy.

This was at variance with much of my training at Old Trafford. In the hard school of Lancashire cricket before the war 'Safety First' had been the watchword. Batsmen by and large - there were notable exceptions like Eddie Paynter - pushed the ball away instead of hitting it hard. With scarcely an exception all the great batsmen of the

REFLECTIONS AND OBSERVATIONS

*past scorned undue restraint in their stroke-play.
Since the force of that conclusion impressed itself
upon my mind it has been my aim, whenever fit
and in form, to take the initiative. A bowler bowls
only as well as the batsman allows him and very
few enjoy having runs scored off them, even only
one or two an over.*

Interestingly, Eddie Paynter has one of the highest
Test Match averages (59.23) of all England players.
Strange to relate he was over 30 years of age before
establishing himself in the Lancashire side.

It seems attacking batting did not always suit.
Remember, Ranjitsinhji was only awarded his 'blue' at
Cambridge University during his final year. As for
Cyril, his new approach made him first choice to open
with Len Hutton in the immediate post war years, a
partnership which was one of England's most
successful pairings.

During the same period, a comment in the Bradman
Albums notes that at the beginning of the tour in April
at Lord's Bradman instructed his '1948 Invincibles' to
take part in a morning of hard hitting practice.

We have already shown how 'playing with a straight
bat' had implications even beyond the cricket field. It
became synonymous with noble, upright behaviour,
firstly with middle class England and then through
connection, with working class cricketers who eventually
became the numerical majority in the game. The culture,
although less pronounced, lingers on to this day, and long
may it last.

BRADMAN REVISITED

However, when Bradman burst onto the scene in the late 1920s, it came as a shock to the English, particularly the cricket-ruling hierarchy. I suspect it was also a shock in Australia - although perhaps less so. How could a country boy from Bowral turn the whole psychology of cricket on its head? Remember Bradman learned to play cricket through his 'solo' game with a golf ball and stump. His idea was simply to control a fast moving ball. In his game there was not a wicket as such to defend, only an area covered by the door behind him.

Throughout his career therefore, Bradman went to the wicket with the scoring of runs as the first consideration. To make matters worse, he stood differently and his bat was not always straight when it should have been. Small wonder Percy Fender (and others) were initially outraged.

So then, Bradman's psychology was different to the norm. There were other aggressive batsmen in cricket history - Gilbert Jessop in the 'golden age' epitomises this intent, but Bradman's achievements have so far exceeded anyone else that, for so long, the style he developed allowing such aggression has remained a mystery. Much easier to be explained away as a 'one off' genius.

Under the circumstances existing in the early Bradman years, it is easy to understand the mentality which made it possible to saddle Harold Larwood with the blame for bodyline bowling. This in spite of England captain Douglas Jardine presenting Larwood with a silver plate inscribed 'from a grateful skipper' for carrying out his instructions and winning the Ashes.

REFLECTIONS AND OBSERVATIONS

It is probable that without Larwood 'bodyline' would have had little impact on the 1932/33 tour. Although 'leg theory', as introduced by Jardine, was used by other bowlers, it was Larwood's extra pace and accuracy which provided the cutting edge. He produced most of the wickets and most of the drama, and in doing so introduced a new dimension to the psychology of batting.

Bradman was aware that he was a prime cause for the introduction of 'bodyline' and therefore its main target, but it's typical of Bradman that over the years he has had little to say about it. Most, if not all, of the furore at the time and subsequently was caused by others. Nonetheless, it left scars which occasionally surfaced.

On the few recorded occasions we have to judge him by, when responding to questions on the subject he gives the impression of regret and some embarrassment. There is an obvious sense of regret that the 'mother country' could adopt methods which seemed to strike at the very heart of the game's ethics. This view was widely held at the time, and not solely by Australians.

I believe the experience hardened Bradman in cricketing terms. Years later, on his final tour of England in 1948, and with those great fast bowlers Lindwall and Miller at his disposal, he was able, within the revised laws, to exact some retribution. It has been well documented by Australian writers, and in particular Jack Fingleton, that he was unsparing of the English batsmen in the use of aggressive short-pitched bowling.

It was, at times, a one-sided bumper war with England unable to respond. He was criticised both at the time and subsequently, but it shows the human side of Bradman which will be readily understood by anyone who has been closely involved in competitive cricket, particularly as a captain.

5.

THE BATTING MACHINE

Don Bradman's performances with his bat ultimately made it quite impossible for anyone in the cricket world to deny his greatness. During most of his career, however, it was rather different. Because his batting did not conform to perceived standards of orthodoxy there were always many ready to denigrate or downgrade his standing. We have told how his technique was variously described as lacking in "grace", "style", "charm", "artistry" - with one critic even describing him as "ugly". Percy Fender, amongst a fistful of criticisms, described an innings as "a mixture of good and bad batting". When his batting feats could finally brook no serious dispute the knockers still persisted. It was fairly generally accepted that, in today's language, he was a "flat-track bully", on which he was a batting machine, but was deemed unable to cope with a sticky wicket.

It is a quirk of human nature, when confronted by proven greatness, to search for an Achilles heel - even invent one if necessary. It is only when such people have passed on from their profession that the thought occurs, Will we ever see their likes again?

Years ago it happened to that great footballer Stanley Matthews, who was accused of overdoing his ball dribbling skills - trying to beat one man too many. For this, he was not only dropped by his country, but also his club. In a more up-to-date context, Pete Sampras, statistically the greatest male tennis player of all time, has been variously described as 'colourless, 'boring', 'machine-like' - amongst other things. All too frequently when proof of sporting greatness has been given beyond a reasonable doubt it cannot be accepted by the critics and officialdom without quite unnecessary quibbling.

With Bradman it was even more so. He had shown the cricket establishments of all interested countries that their 'correct' way of batting not only was not the only way to bat, but not necessarily even the best way of batting. This proved to be too much for many English 'experts' who, though eventually accepting his 'genius', found it better to explain him away as a 'one-off genius'.

One of the speakers at the Bradman 'Symposium' at Lord's in June 2000, Richard Holt, Research Professor at De Montfort University, Leicester, even went as far as to say that in his research, there was, in England, a North/South divide on the subject. The point made was that Bradman was much more a cricketing hero in the North and was viewed with much more circumspection in the South. Perhaps it was a simple matter that the 'Lord's influence' was less apparent in the counties of Lancashire and Yorkshire, who both honoured him with life membership. In Yorkshire particularly, scene of many of his triumphs, he was always accepted, without reservation, for his achievements alone, and was highly popular with most of the public (try telling a 'Tyke' that Bradman was unorthodox and lacked style/charm; the likely answer would have been "look in t' scorebook lad").

Although this picture is from a testimonial match it illustrates perfectly a facet of Bradman for which he was renowned and was the subject of frequent comment. His half-smile gives the relaxed impression of a man at ease with himself and confident he will prevail.

Bradman's style opens up the leg side for his famed pull through mid-wicket. He is in total control as he plays the ball powerfully to ground.

This ferocious hook, backwards of square, shows versatility, freedom of movement and balance, and is unlikely to be replicated from an orthodox batting position.

For this leg side stroke, Bradman demonstrates the process of rolling the wrists. This is inherently a part of his batting style and means the ball is automatically played to ground, a feature common to all of Bradman's attacking shots.

Everything about this picture illustrates co-ordination and balance. Of particular interest is the obvious use of hands and wrists in making a complete follow through.

Yards down the wicket, Bradman is still perfectly balanced
for this drive through the offside. It was this kind of footwork
which so intimidated the bowlers of his era.

In the Long Room at Lord's.
Pictured is author Tony Shillinglaw (right) with co-writer
Brian Hale in the Long Room, Lord's, at the Bradman
Symposium. They were rather amused to find the portrait of
Sir Donald Bradman (top) coupled with Douglas Jardine. Sir
Leonard Hutton looks on over Tony's left shoulder.

The memory of Don Bradman should not only take the form of records and memorabilia. My belief is that the acceptance and the adoption of his 'Rotary' batting style by future generations of batsmen would provide the true and lasting legacy of Sir Donald Bradman as his gift to the game of cricket.

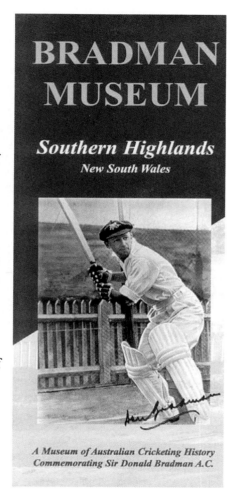

BRADMAN MUSEUM

Southern Highlands
New South Wales

A Museum of Australian Cricketing History
Commemorating Sir Donald Bradman A.C.

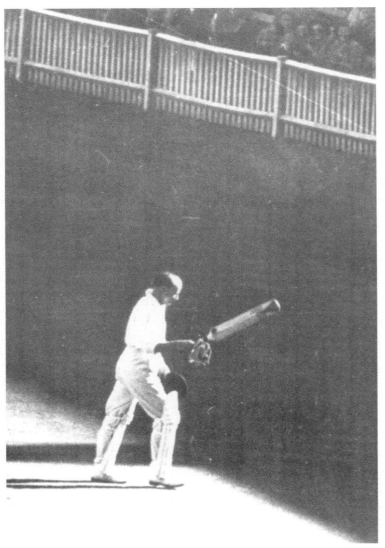

In this evocative picture from his last match at Sydney in 1949, Bradman heads off into the shadows of mystery - where his batting has remained ever since. I hope by the time the reader has finished this book at least some of those shadows will have been lifted.

REFLECTIONS AND OBSERVATIONS

It is appropriate therefore to let Bill Bowes, Yorkshire fast bowler who played many times during the Ashes series of the 1930s, have the last say on Bradman's all wicket capabilities:

It was at Sheffield in the 1930 season that I first met Bradman. His reputation had been established during the 1928 season; nonetheless George Macauley, after a couple of balls told me, 'I shall get this chap caught and bowled'. He did, but on a wicket very nearly 'sticky', Don scored 70 odd.

Of a similar wicket at Sydney during the 1932/1933 tour, Hedley Verity, the greatest 'sticky' wicket bowler in the game, said after pressing his thumb into the soft yielding surface, 'poor Don'. But 'poor Don' again scored 70 and it was Wally Hammond's off spinner which eventually accounted for him. (Bradman in fact scored 71 out of a total of 128 all out).

Bradman would have played better than anybody else on a corrugated iron roof. On 'sticky' wickets, on all wickets hard or soft, against bowlers fast, medium or slow, against spinners or swingers, he never had an equal.

Justice however was finally served at Lord's. Besides being offered the presidency of the MCC - which logistics forced him to turn down. Bradman's portrait now hangs in the Long Room. It is in a corner, paired with a portrait of Douglas Jardine!

6.

RHYTHM AND CO-ORDINATION

With few exceptions, the greatest sportsmen/women, whatever their game, develop a smooth rhythm and easy co-ordination which sustains them over many years of performance, thereby helping to establish their reputations. This fluency of movement enables them to appear natural performers, thus making their art appear 'easy'.

The great Indian slow bowler, Bishan Bedi, had this to say about movement:

Look after your action. Treasure it. Work at it daily to preserve your rhythm, because if you do that most things will fall into place and develop properly. Think of an action as having a beginning, a middle and an end. The run-up; a poised delivery side-ways on with head looking over the leading shoulder; and the follow through. Some bowlers only manage two of the three. Remember the action is not complete until all three are in place.

Tony Lewis, writing about Bishan Bedi in the MCC's 'Masterclass', gave this picturesque description of his action:

REFLECTIONS AND OBSERVATIONS

When you have seen Bishan Bedi twirl down his left arm spinners after 60 overs with the same gentle rhythm and control as he settled into at the start of his spell, you understand why he is a great bowling action. Even more so in his own country, where the test of stamina is more severe in burning heat and on baked grounds which tug on the muscles and jar on the joints.

I have always thought that a great clockmaker would have been proud to have set Bedi in motion - a mechanism finely balanced, cogs rolling silently and hands sweeping in smooth arcs across the face. Yet it would be wrong to portray him as something less than human - all hardware and no heart, because he bowls with a fiery aggression which belies his genial nature.

I am sure something similar could be written about many of the truly great bowlers. Rhythm and co-ordination being the major factor in their success. By extension, it is also equally true in other sports.

Bedi talks of his action having three elements - run-up, delivery and follow through, all of which merge into one completely smooth co-ordinated whole. The smooth flow of Bradman's stroke play can similarly be said to comprise three elements - pick-up, stroke and follow-through. In both cases the very repetitive smoothness of their actions became a habit through long practice in and out of competition. This reduces the elements of strain and is much less physically and mentally tiring.

BRADMAN REVISITED

Many good judges consider Alan Knott to be England's best post-war wicket-keeper. In MCC's 'Masterclass' he gives an interesting pen picture of how he kept wicket. Standing in a crouched position with his hands low between his legs, he started to rock forward onto the balls of his feet so that he came out of his stance into a balanced position just before the bowler delivered the ball. He finishes by saying:

It is not only your hands that take the ball. Your whole body takes it in a rhythm off the pitch.

Once again this description could easily be adapted to describe Bradman preparing to make a stroke. I am sure it could also be applied to other great players but the significant point is the importance placed on rhythm, co-ordination and balance, all leading to good timing. Bradman seemed to have developed, and combined, the reactions and instincts of a great wicket-keeper with the rhythm and control of a great bowler.

Occasionally a sportsman comes along who throws away the rule book and proves he can play the game a different way. In the world of athletics many will remember with surprise - even shock - when Dick Fosbury burst onto the scene, winning the 1968 Olympic high jump title with his sensational 'Fosbury Flop'. He changed the event literally overnight when it was realised that his new method had greater possibilities than any other method so far tried. There is now, it seems, no other way to jump if you wish to compete with a chance of winning. It is a different

REFLECTIONS AND OBSERVATIONS

method but still reliant on rhythm, co-ordination and balance.

In a similar if less obvious way, Bradman, with his different stance, grip, back-lift and attitude, offered a different way of batting. He went on to prove that, for him at least, existing performance parameters counted for nothing. He moved them onto an altogether different level. The surprising fact is that in the 70 years or so since he illustrated this new approach - unlike the Fosbury case - no one attempted to copy him. Even more surprisingly, no in depth attempt has been made to study how he did it.

We have shown how great players like Bradman, Bedi and Knott, in explaining themselves, tend to emphasise the human rather than the technical aspects. Bradman in particular was always quick to advise that natural development should precede theory, in this way rhythm, balance and co-ordination are in place before thoughts are directed into technical matters or the theory of stroke play.

7.

LEARNING THE LESSONS

After Don Bradman finished playing first class cricket in 1949, he remained closely associated with the game, becoming chairman of the Australian Test Selectors, a post he finally relinquished, for health reasons, in 1971. He was therefore at the very top of Australian cricket, player and administrator, for an unrivalled 45 years. In the cricket world he became for the 20th century what W.G. Grace had been for the 19th century. As a batsman, he established figures that nobody else has even approached. His death on the 25th February 2001 caused headlines and major coverage in all the cricket playing countries - even though more than 50 years had elapsed since his last appearance at the wicket in a serious game.

Don Bradman was not a recluse, but he shunned publicity, preferring to live a quiet family life, refusing for the most part even to give official interviews. However, fortunately for posterity, he relented, allowing Ray Martin an interview to commemorate his 87th birthday for Australian TV. Ray Martin and his team should be congratulated for the result. It was an astonishing performance for a man of his years. Viewers, young and old alike, could only look on in admiration, perhaps wonderment, at the resultant display of modesty, astuteness, quick thinking and more than a hint of iron

REFLECTIONS AND OBSERVATIONS

resolve. Ray Martin bowled him questions, and the great Don placed his answers at will around the studio just as adeptly as he once played a cricket ball. It was a *tour de force* quite in keeping with the image of a truly great cricketer.

Bradman himself never claimed to be the greatest batsman. Throughout his career he just continually produced the goods and left the talking to others. He did produce his memoirs and a book, 'The Art of Cricket', explaining his methods and the basics of batting, as he saw them, but that was that. It was for others to take notice or otherwise. Nobody appeared to give them serious attention: quite the reverse. He was seen to perform differently and in a manner less aesthetically attractive. His success was explained away as having physical causes relating to speed, reflexes, super eyesight, stamina and perhaps mental ones also, such as concentration and determination.

It was therefore more a mixture of such 'natural advantages' which produced this one-off genius. This pretty much holds sway in many quarters today. It is a comfortable viewpoint which allows the belief that Bradman's achievements were despite his technique, not because of it. This view, as we have shown, is at odds with the facts. Any study of Bradman's health and eyesight shows his amazing feats were accomplished in spite of barely average eyesight and, for a great sportsman, pretty indifferent health for much of his sporting life.

Perhaps the most significant finding regarding the early career of Don Bradman, is the fact that up to the time of averaging over a hundred in his first full season of club cricket at Bowral at the age of seventeen, he had only ever played eight innings and scored 375 runs. It is clear that his all-round skills and method were both fashioned and highly developed before he ever picked up a bat in earnest competition.

This indicates that by understanding and implementing the principles of his distinctive early development, enormous benefit may be offered to future generations of batsmen. It must be emphasised that technique never entered into Bradman's early development - which centred solely on controlling a fast, erratic moving ball.

The second most significant finding concerning the early Bradman is the fact that, by his own admission, he had no contact with first class cricket before his first season with New South Wales. He had read no books by great cricketers and, with the exception of a portion of two day's play in a Test Match, had seen no first class cricket at all. He was, in fact, the epitome of the uncoached, untaught natural cricketer.

It is hard to envisage such natural cricketers as Bradman and Hobbs emerging today. In England, establishment figures, politicians, pundits and other interested parties instinctively call for more money to provide academies and more coaches in the belief that this will solve the problem. To date, it shows no signs of doing so despite years of the increased centralisation of coaching, which has produced national coaching books and videos.

If anything, the situation has deteriorated. In the Ashes year of 2001 the Australians could produce a full batting

REFLECTIONS AND OBSERVATIONS

second eleven, any of whom would be virtually guaranteed a place in the England team, whereas few English batsmen could be considered for Australia. Something is obviously wrong. A variety of reasons have been proffered, high amongst them being criticism of the County Championship. It has produced great players for generations - even in the days of uncovered pitches, and today, unlike 30 or 40 years ago, the best bowlers of all the cricket playing nations become contracted players for County teams. It is also worth pointing out that small 'new' cricket playing countries, like Zimbabwe, are producing outstanding batsmen despite a very restricted, some would say weak, structure.

Cricket, by its very nature, lends itself to complication and theory, and today's technical coverage, in particular by television and video, can easily lead to the belief that teaching a set technique can be a straightforward answer to improving batsmanship. The dictionary tells us that technique is "the mechanical part of art". This "mechanical part" is now getting so complicated that there is an increasing use of psychologists in an attempt to sort things out. The great South African golfer, Gary Player, called his whole process "paralysis by analysis".

Perhaps now is the time to revert back more to the 'artistic' side of cricket. Both Bradman and Hobbs expressed their belief that the way they learned to play the game was of fundamental importance to their development. This entailed constant practice with a ball, not structured movement. Formalised coaching played no part in their early years. There is something important to consider here.

BRADMAN REVISITED

We have already shown that Bradman's early development owed much to his 'golf ball and stump' game, developing a style which was perhaps unique. According to his partner over many years, Jack Fingleton, it was unique. Bradman struck a blow for individuality in batting which should never be far from the thoughts of a good coach. His style posed serious questions about batting theory which have not been satisfactorily resolved to this day.

Bradman's stance at the wicket is discouraged by today's coaches who, as illustrated in MCC's Masterclass video, teach young players to stand with their bat open-faced behind their rear foot. This is based on the over-simplified principle that a bat which goes straight back will come straight down. Standing in this manner, the bat has only one natural initial movement - backwards. This movement tends to fix the shoulders and shift the weight to the back foot.

Bradman's initial movement was very different and resulted from his grip on the bat held 'closed faced' between his feet. From this position the bat can only naturally move outwards away from the body - so bringing him onto the toes of both feet, a position of perfect balance for either forward or backward movement.

From this position, in making attacking strokes, Bradman's bat would describe a smooth 'rotary' movement with complete follow through using the same kind of motion he developed for his golf ball and stump game.

It is clear therefore that Bradman's initial movement is different to that being taught today. It is also true that many of the great batsmen of the past did not take their bats straight back in their initial movement. We have quoted Alec Bedser saying that all the great batsmen he bowled to took their initial movement towards "at least second slip". This is backed up by Geoffrey Boycott, who says "it is not a natural movement". Bradman himself says the 'straight back' technique is more restrictive to attacking strokes. These are good grounds for thinking therefore that there are serious questions to be answered on the subject. The most important being, are we teaching young players a method which is too restrictive?

Perhaps too much emphasis is being given to defending straight balls to the detriment of scoring runs.

The timing of Bradman's movement is equally crucial. There is no doubt that, although he stood unusually still until the last possible moment, his initial movements were always before the ball started on its path. Bradman is categorical on this point. Indeed his great feats would not have otherwise been possible. His compact stillness misled many good judges - but we have already shown the difficulties of forming a judgement on this issue. Suffice to repeat that even with today's technology it is very difficult to pick up.

In the introduction to this book we stated our objective was to explain why Sir Donald Bradman was statistically so superior to other batsmen, so that his methods of both development and technique could be understood, accepted and offered to future generations of batsmen. It is not about producing another Bradman, but about offering youngsters the additional scope of his scoring methods.

BRADMAN REVISITED

In a commemorative edition of the Sydney Morning Herald to honour Sir Donald Bradman's 90th birthday, Ray Martin asked former team mate and partner Bill Brown two questions:

1. What made Bradman so much better than everyone else?
2. What really was his secret?

In answering, Bill Brown told of Bradman's speed of movement and certainty of batting, and went on to give some illustrations. Philip Derriman, commenting in the Herald, thought somehow the question was left in the air and did not get to the heart of the matter. The best short answer to both questions is suggested from our investigation. His 'rotary' method, played from a position of perfect balance, allowed him to become arguably the best co-ordinated player in the game's history. His success owed much less than is supposed to eyesight or physical fitness, as there is little doubt that many of cricket's great batsmen were at least a match for him in this respect without getting near to his amazing figures.

We have paid tribute to his strength of character and determination, but only total belief in the unfettered development and method he evolved could have given Bradman the supreme confidence for which he was famous. Very early in his career he experimented with the 'orthodox' approach, both grip and stance, and rejected them for his own preferences. Not for Bradman cricket talk of mind and theory, for him experience, born of hard work and practice and based upon control of the ball, was always the likeliest path to success. The psychology of sport is known to be a subject to which Bradman gave little credence, which is in keeping with his modest outlook and straightforward batting philosophy. The best advice Bradman had for an outgoing batsman was "watch the ball and concentrate".

I have, I hope, explained how Bradman did it. I have also shown that his method, if 'unorthodox', was sound. That it can be copied is apparent - there is no secret. The combination of factors which produced Bradman may not be repeated, but this does not mean we cannot learn from his early development which led to such mastery of a cricket ball.

A short time ago Michael Parkinson, the well-known TV presenter and journalist, wrote the following article in the Daily Telegraph:

> *The other day I was talking to Jeff Thomson, the Australian fast bowler, about Bradman, and Jeff said that in the 1970s he was at a social event organised by a man who owned a cricket field. During the afternoon, Sir Donald, in his 60s by then, was approached by two young cricketers who were on the fringe of the State team. They asked him if they could bowl at him. He pointed out that he had not played for 30 years, but eventually removed his jacket and picked up a bat.*
>
> *At first the young men bowled respectfully at him, aware both of his age and the fact that he had neither pads nor gloves. But when Bradman started*

playing shots, they quickened up and eventually were bowling flat out. According to Thomson, the quicker they bowled, the harder Bradman smote them to the boundary.

Jeff said, 'It was bloody magnificent. All my life I had looked at his record and thought - how can anyone be twice as good as Greg Chappell? That day I found out.'

8.

THE LEGACY

When comparing Don Bradman's batting style with the orthodox approach it is important to understand that the differences are fundamental. From the moment Bradman began lifting his bat the execution of his strokes took on a synchronised motion of their own. The basis of this movement being rotation of hips, shoulders, arms and wrists extending into the rotary action of his bat. From start to finish the movement is smooth and continuous.

I was only to gradually appreciate the full meaning of this when, at the end of my own career, I began to study Bradman. I now remember with regret how, many years previously, I had changed my own style, at the age of 15 years, on the instructions of my first coach. At this age I had been selected to open for the North of England versus the South, having instinctively adopted the Bradman style from the outset (unaware, of course, of any association). Throughout my career, despite some success, I never felt totally comfortable when batting. It never occurred to me to question the wisdom of coaching and orthodoxy. I came to understand, much too late, that my original instinctive batting style had given me an inner confidence and freedom that I was never again to fully recapture. It thus became more important to me than ever that I should try to promote a much broader approach to batting technique. I believe Bradman's style should be offered to all - not as dogma - but an option. It is well to remember Bradman's message that the success he achieved would not have been possible using orthodox techniques.

My feelings were reinforced when, at the conclusion of my playing days, I undertook an official coaching course. I discontinued after the first stage in the belief that batting should be less dogmatic and theoretical and more natural. More like Bradman and Hobbs. This experience increased my desire to study and learn. It has been a long journey.

I believe a good starting point to help young batsmen are these ten extracts from Don Bradman's book 'The Art of Cricket':

1. I cannot emphasise too much my belief that 'watching the ball' and 'concentration' are of greater importance than all the theories.

2. I would counsel every boy who is interested in batting to play with a ball at every opportunity. Whether it be a golf ball, tennis ball, baseball or any other kind, it does not matter. It will help train the eye and co-ordinate brain, eye and muscle.

3. It is a mistake to fog a boy's mind with a multiplicity of complicated instructions, which means he forgets the much more important and simple basic principles.

4. The basic technique of the straight bat is sound for defence. However, there should be all possible emphasis on attack, on the aggressive outlook, and if technique is going to prove the master of a player and not his servant, then it will not be doing its job.

REFLECTIONS AND OBSERVATIONS

5. Coaching should deal with what to do with the ball not so much as how to do it.

6. Better to hit the ball with an apparently unorthodox style than to miss it with a 'correct' one.

7. To be given the opportunity plus the desire to learn are the keys to success.

8. I don't care who the player is or how great his skill, there is no substitute for proper practice.

9. Watch others, note their methods and learn by observation and example.

10. In the final analysis the best teacher is yourself. Analyse things sensibly. Work out what suits you personally. Practice and observe.

We should learn from Bradman in the same way that Tiger Woods learned to play golf as reported by Frank Malley in the Daily Post. Woods revealed he practised between four and twelve hours each day between tournaments and based his meticulous preparation on Jack Nicklaus, because "if it was good enough for the greatest player who ever lived it is good enough for me".

On this basis if Tiger had taken up cricket he would have found out everything Bradman did and learned from it. There is no reason why any budding young batsman could not adopt a similar attitude. Unfortunately, with our centralised coaching system such a situation would be stifled at birth. Although the most recent amendment to the MCC coaching manual adopts a more flexible approach to batting, the very minute a young player is told to stand with his bat open-faced behind his rear foot, the battle is lost. From this position the only natural movement is straight back. Bradman's style of batting cannot be adopted from this stance.

The supreme confidence of his style, which so often enabled him to go from 100 to 200 plus, was often referred to by sports writers and critics as the 'killer instinct'. The Right Reverend David Sheppard, former England opener, besides subsequently Bishop of Liverpool, used the expression when kindly replying to one of my letters. Yet, in the animal kingdom, it is used to describe one of superior size, strength, speed and ferocity, hunting down its prey. Bradman, of course, had none of these attributes, which leaves us with the obvious question, and answer. His supreme confidence was based upon the ability his practice and style allowed him.

Unlike many players Bradman never had cause to seriously think about changing his style. His consistency never made it necessary. When first arriving on the scene he resisted attempts made to change him to a more orthodox approach - but not before first experimenting for himself. He simply decided that his method was best for him.

That Bradman made batting instinctive is illustrated by the rather amusing story of his tour of the U.S.A and Canada.

In 1932 Arthur Mailey arranged for an Australian team to make this tour but it was made clear to him that the necessary financial backing would only be available if Bradman was a member of the party. Bradman had just married and agreed to go only if his wife Jessie could accompany him. This was agreed and the result was a highly successful tour. Mr and Mrs Bradman enjoyed their honeymoon, and cricket wives please note, Don scored 3779 runs at an average of 102.10, with a top score of 260.

Making allowances for weak opposition, it is clear that circumstances had little effect on Bradman. Concentration was a habit and the method he had evolved meant he addressed every ball in the same manner and instinctively reacted accordingly.

I believe that if a batsman develops a style which is successful it is best to leave well alone. Most batsmen go through bad spells that can usually be put down to the luck of the game, good balls or just bad judgement. Tinkering with their method is rarely the answer. Doing this generally leads to a lack of conviction and more inconsistency. If a batsman does change his style successfully it is probably because his style had serious limitations.

There is an example of a successful batsman changing a very successful style and it is worth considering. In the early 1930s, with Bradman already established as the outstanding scorer of his era, he did have one serious rival. Most people in both England and Australia consider this to be Walter Hammond. We don't know much about Hammond's early batting style but Bill Frindall described him as such:

Hammond was a Dover-born son of a soldier who cut his cricketing teeth in China, and against a wicket chalked on a gun shed in Malta. In 1923 he launched his professional career with scores of 110 and 92 against Surrey and soon established himself

BRADMAN REVISITED

*as an audacious but polished hitter, an impulsive
hooker of the fastest bowling and a ferocious driver.*

In his book 'Cricketer's School' Hammond revealed
how the words of an England selector caused him to
change his style and limit his on-side stroke-making. As
a young man already well on the road to success he was
playing against Lancashire at Old Trafford. In
Hammond's own words: "I was able to see the ball very
clearly that day and I hit up 250 not out at a fast rate
largely from leg-side shots." Later it came to his attention
that an England selector watching the game had remarked
to Neville Cardus, "That boy will never play for England,
he is far too reckless." Hammond wrote: "I decided to
improve my off-side play and reduce my leg-side shots so
that I could play for England."

Unfortunately we do not know whether Hammond
received any serious coaching as a boy or young man, but
given his background it seems unlikely. Perhaps he was
another in the Bradman/Hobbs tradition of self-taught
players; but this admittedly is speculation.

What is not speculation is that the Aussies recognised
Hammond as an off-side player. When a player is so
characterised at any level of cricket the bowlers bowl and set
their fields accordingly - which is, of course, what the
Australians did. Whether the unknown England selector did
Hammond any favours with his comments provides room for
thought. But standing in the slips watching Bradman plunder
the leg-side must have given Hammond cause for reflection.

Fortunately for the cricket world Bradman had no such
distractions or doubts. It is difficult to conceive of any

sportsman more confident in his own ability and it has been argued that no other sportsman so dominated his chosen sport in terms of figures and performances. Despite this, to my knowledge no cricket authority has been prepared to scientifically study or adopt the method he made so successful.

In his book 'The Best of the Best', Melbourne scientist Charles Davis submits a comparative study of Bradman's performances in relation to other great batsmen, and indeed, outstanding sportsmen in many other fields.

Although a fascinating exercise in statistics, the author's explanation for Bradman's statistical superiority appears to fall back on supposed psychological advantages without consideration to method.

Bradman's self belief was certainly a major part of his greatness but this was based upon a total confidence in his own unique batting method allied to dedicated practice. Without this, any supposed psychological advantages would be meaningless.

In modern parlance, any player must first be able to 'walk the walk' before being able to 'talk the talk'. Perhaps today's lack of consideration for this basic concept is why Don Bradman gave such little credence to the psychology of sport.

Attempting to change entrenched views on batting, particularly in England, is extremely difficult. It was Bradman's golf ball and stump game that developed his natural movement and concentration. He carried his approach into competitive cricket from the very beginning; his stance at the wicket was part of this and was fundamental to his success. Anyone wishing to follow his style would have to, at the very least, adopt a similar grip and stance. Herein lies the problem. Almost as soon as a young player gets his first instruction, he will be guided into placing his bat, open faced, behind his rear foot. From the outset he is therefore denied the full scope and facility of Bradman's stroke play.

Bradman has left us with his legacy. I believe the legacy is to change this thinking.

These studies have led me to conclude that the introduction of Bradman's methods into mainstream consideration can only have a beneficial effect. This could prove to be the most important development since the early pioneers led by W.G. Grace first popularised the modern form of batting from both front and back foot.

9.

POSTSCRIPT

Just prior to going to print, my attention has been drawn to a report in The Sydney Morning Herald of a leading Australian cricket coach who wishes to install a tank stand at the New South Wales coaching centre.

In the meantime he has young players repeating a version of Bradman's boyhood game against a wall with a table-tennis bat and ball. The coach is reported as saying: "I suspect the golf ball game had a lot to do with Bradman's hand-eye co-ordination." This statement has now fairly general acceptance. It is not however the end of the matter, which is what is suggested by boys being trained one-handed with a table-tennis bat and ball as a means to quicken their reactions.

The important difference is that Bradman gripped his stump (ie his makeshift bat) with both hands. As a result he not only developed brain, eye and muscle co-ordination to an extraordinary degree but also, as a consequence, a continual 'Rotary' motion of the stump in order to control the erratic fast-moving ball.

All bodily movements - that is, wrists, arms shoulders, hips and feet - became automatically a part of this function. Crucially, Bradman's form of game developed the mental and physical 'as one' and it is wrong to assume that in Bradman these can be viewed separately.

BRADMAN REVISITED

In the same Sydney Morning Herald article Richard Mulvaney, Chief Executive of the Bradman Museum, expressed a wish that as far as Bradman was concerned "the inexplicable needs to be explained and we should do it sooner rather than later." Mr Mulvaney went on to say that people looking into the phenomenon have generally come to one of three conclusions:

1 That he owed his success to freakish natural talent.
2 That he owed his success to the mental powers that enabled him to make maximum use of the talent he had.
3 That he owed his success to a unique practical formula for success he stumbled upon.

My view is that in his boyhood game Don Bradman stumbled upon a unique practical formula for success, while at the same time developing and harnessing the mental powers that enabled him to make the maximum use of the great natural talent he appeared to have.

As previously stated, Bradman's secret was to develop the Mental and Physical AS ONE.

After much study and with the results now in book form, I believe that I have covered all the important factors which contributed to making Don Bradman the acknowledged greatest batsman of them all.

I do not claim that there is nothing more to say on the subject; for a start, Professor Lees' experiments on movement and balance in the making of cricket strokes were not completed, but I believe I understand the approach and method which made Bradman's pre-eminence possible, and trust that I have explained this to the satisfaction of my readers. Equally importantly, I am quite sure that this can be taught successfully - preferably to young players at the beginning of their careers.

How and why Bradman developed his unique batting style is just as important as appreciating the finished article. Bradman can only be studied 'as a whole'. There is a tendency for interested observers to over-analyse the parts and, by so doing, take away or complicate natural movement. Rather like trying to isolate and separate Fred Astaire's head, arm and feet movement in order to replicate them in other dancers. Bradman's stance at the wicket is very much a reflection of his boyhood game with golf ball and stump which gave him masterly control over a moving ball. This was the position which gave him the balance and easy movement for his full range of shots.

With this lesson very much in mind I introduced the Bradman way of batting to a group of 12 year olds at a school where I am given freedom to experiment alongside the more traditional approach. I am excited by the early indications but it is far too soon to enlarge on this at the present time. The very first lesson in batting (or any sport) is that there are no short cuts to success. This can only be obtained by long hours of practice, regardless of natural ability and whatever style or method is adopted. This is the first lesson for aspiring batsmen.

The Bradman, or, as I have termed it, the 'rotary' style of movement, after practice, offers a sense of freedom to both mind and body. Because it is repetitive it is less tiring. All movement is induced by the batting grip and the stance at the wicket. During the course of my studies I returned to this style of batting for the first time since, as a 15 year old, I had allowed a well-meaning coach to change me into a 'mass produced' orthodox batsman. I regret very much not being strong enough to resist. It is my sincere hope that future generations will be allowed the choice. I will continue to work towards this end.

I hope that my analysis will open up a debate on the very nature of 'orthodoxy' in batting and as a consequence budding young cricketers will be able to develop their natural talents free from dogma.

In the introduction to his book, 'How To Play Cricket', Bradman wrote:

I do hope the value of my experience will be within the reach of everybody.

It is time for cricket to respect this wish as a lasting tribute to the world's most successful batsman.

APPENDIX 1

BRADMAN'S FIRST CLASS CRICKET CAREER

IN AUSTRALIA

Season	Inns	NO	HS	Runs	Ave	100s
1927-28	10	1	134	416	46.22	2
1928-29	24	6	*340 (a)	1,690	93.88	7
1929-30	16	2	*452	1,586	113.28	5
1930-31	18	-	258	1,422	79.00	5
1931-32	13	1	*299	1,403	116.91	7
1932-33	21	2	238	1,171	61.63	3
1933-34	11	2	253	1,192	132.44	5
1934-35	Did not play					
1935-36	9	-	369	1,173	130.33	4
1936-37	19	1	270	1,552	86.22	6
1937-38	18	2	246	1,437	89.81	7
1938-39	7	1	225	919	153.16	6
1939-40	15	3	267	1,475	122.91	5
1940-41	4	-	12	18	4.50	0
1945-46	3	1	112	232	116.00	1
1946-47	14	1	234	1,032	79.38	4
1947-48	12	2	201	1,296	129.60	(b)8
1948-49	4	-	123	216	54.00	1

IN ENGLAND

Season	Inns	NO	HS	Runs	Ave	100s
1930	36	6	334	(c)2,960	98.66	10
1934	27	3	304	2,020	84.16	7
1938	26	5	278	2,429	115.66	(d)13

1948	31	4	187	2,428	89.92	11
TOTAL	**338**	**43**	***452**	**28,067**	**95.14**	**117**

(a) 1,690 Record aggregate for an Australian season.
(b) 8 Record number of centuries for an Australian season.
(c) 2,960 Record aggregate for an Australian in England.
(d) 13 Record number of centuries for an Australian in an English season.

IN TEST CRICKET

Season	Inns	NO	HS	Runs	Ave	100s
England	63	7	334	5,028	89.78	19
W. Indies	6	-	223	447	74.50	2
S. Africa	5	1	*299	806	201.50	4
India	6	2	201	715	178.75	4
TOTAL	**80**	**10**	**334**	**6,996**	**99.94**	**29**

STATISTICAL SUMMARY OF SIR DONALD BRADMAN'S CAREER

	Inns	NO	HS	Agg	Ave
All Matches	669	107	*452	50,731	90.27
All 1st-class	338	43	*452	28,067	95.1
All 2nd-class	331	64	*320	22,664	84.8
All Test Cricket	80	10	334	6,996	99.9
Tests v England	63	7	334	5,028	89.78
Sheffield Shield	96	15	*452	8,926	110.19
Grade Cricket	93	17	303	6,598	86.8

Numbers of centuries scored
All Matches 211
All First-Class Matches. 117
All Test Cricket 29
Tests v England 19

Sheffield Shield Matches 36
Grade Cricket 28

Of the 211 centuries, 41 were double centuries, 8 treble centuries and one a quadruple century.

Methods of dismissal

Number of innings 669
Caught 340
Bowled 148
Not out 107
L.B.W. 37
Stumped 22
Run out 14
Hit wicket 1

WITH HIS UNIQUE STANCE, BRADMAN COULD SCORE HIS RUNS TO ALL PARTS OF THE FIELD

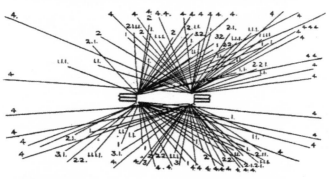

Defying the purists: Bradman could still hit the ball anywhere, as shown in this chart of his 334 runs at Leeds in the Third Test in 1930.

APPENDIX 2

THE BRADMAN STYLE

To anyone wishing to pass on the Bradman style to youngsters, the following basic principles are suggested:

1. Briefly explain Don Bradman's standing as a batsman.

2. Introduce pupils to Bradman's closed-face grip and stance.

3. Point out that the orthodox and Bradman batting styles are fundamentally different.

4. To avoid confusion, pupil and helper must decide which method is to be adopted in the same way as bowlers need to choose between the contrasting feel and motion of side-on and front-on bowling.

5. Ensure the relaxing of elbows and knees. Should the arms be straight, the shoulders become rigid so greatly restricting footwork and body motion.

6. Encourage pupils to keep head and bat still as the bowler approaches.

7. For beginners, recommend the instructor stands behind the wicket encouraging the batsman to begin lifting the bat gently prior to release of the ball.

8. From this position it is remarkable how often the ball is hit, which is the first thing a beginner wishes to do.

9. Because the feet are balanced and the bat is free and moving, instinct takes over on sighting the ball.

10. At this stage it is unlikely the hits will conform to the present text books. However, pupils with aptitude and aggressive intent can hit the ball surprisingly hard through their use of the wrists and footwork.

APPENDIX 3

A REPORT ON A PRELIMINARY INVESTIGATION OF THE ORTHODOX AND BRADMAN BATTING TECHNIQUES

Liverpool John Moores University
Centre for Sport and Exercise sciences
Biomechanics Department

by Professor Adrian Lees

INTRODUCTION

The purpose of this investigation was to use the high speed motion analysis system at Liverpool John Moores University to investigate whether the Bradman technique for batting could be considered to be at least equal to the Orthodox technique when fulfilling the basic principles of batsmanship.

The investigation is preliminary in that it does not control for a number of variables (for example ball speed, pitch, spin, etc) and was performed in a laboratory setting where, although a realistic stroke could be played, did not equate to field or net play. Further because of time involved in collecting, processing and analysing data, just two subjects were used, one who was proficient in the Orthodox technique and one who was able to demonstrate both techniques.

BRADMAN REVISITED

DATA COLLECTION

The ProReflex motion analysis system was used to collect three-dimensional positions of the main body joints as illustrated below. In addition three points were located on the bat. The data were collected at 240 Hz (samples per second). Illustrations of the data collection environment are given below.

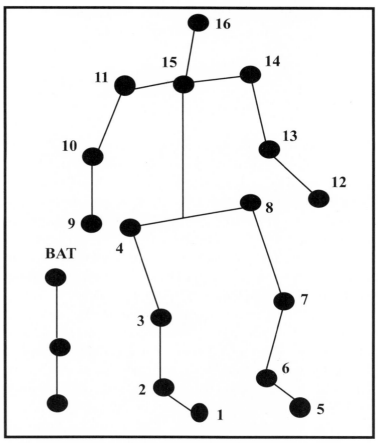

BRADMAN REVISITED

Two batters were used. One (TS) was able to perform both the orthodox and Bradman techniques, and one (PH) was able to perform the Orthodox technique. For each data record a ball was bowled to the batter who played the most appropriate stroke. Several strokes were recorded from each batter covering a range of shots, typically front foot drives, back foot drives, pulls and cuts.

Each recorded shot was later analysed and several variables were recorded. One was the time taken from initiation of bat lift to ball strike, another was the maximum speed of the bat at around impact. Other variables were available as well as a qualitative inspection of the strokes but for brevity are not reported here.

RESULTS

Data for the time of bat lift to impact(s) and the peak bat speed before striking the ball are given in the table below. It can be seen that there is variation between the performances of the same stroke for each batter. In general there is no discernable difference in either variable between batter or between techniques.

STROKE	PH-ORTHODOX		TS-ORTHODOX		TS-BRADMAN	
	Time(s)	Speed(m/s)	Time(s)	Speed (m/s)	Time(s)	Speed (m/s)
BF DRIVE	1.04	12.4	0.90	15.8	1.10	13.2
BF DRIVE			1.14	13.8		
BF DRIVE			1.20	13.5		
FF DRIVE	1.14	12.8	1.08	14.2	1.01	13.0
FF DRIVE	0.93	11.7	0.89	15.2		

PULL	0.98	13.4		0.83	17.5	0.84	19.0
PULL				0.79	16.9	1.14	18.2
PULL				0.78	14.3		
Late CUT	1.52	7.2	...			1.14	11.4
Late CUT			...			1.08	9.8

CONCLUSIONS

1. The Bradman technique appears to have no disadvantages over the orthodox technique in terms of time to complete stroke and speed of bat at impact.

2. From a qualitative inspection of the strokes used it is clear that both techniques allow the bat to gain a vertical orientation at the start of the downsweep into impact with the ball.

3. The above conclusions are drawn from limited data under realistic but laboratory conditions. Further investigation of the two techniques is warranted under more controlled conditions.

4. There are other aspects to batting technique worthy of further investigation. These include (a) the use of the elbow and wrist in orientating the bat prior to and during the downsweep, and (b) the balance associated with each technique in terms of ease with which the transition into a particular stroke can be made.

BIBLIOGRAPHY

BOOKS:

How To Play Cricket, Sir Donald Bradman
(Daily Mail)
The Art of Cricket, Sir Donald Bradman
(Hodder & Stoughton)
Farewell To Cricket, Sir Donald Bradman
(Hodder & Stoughton)
The Bradman Albums
(Queen Anne Press)
Bradman The Great, B.J. Wakely
(Mainstream Publishing)
Wisden Cricketers' Almanack (various years)
(John Wisden & Co. Ltd.)
MCC Masterclass
(Weidenfeld & Nicholson)
A History of Cricket, H.S. Altham & E.W. Altham
(Allen & Unwin)
Express Deliveries, Bill Bowes
(Stanley Paul & Co. Ltd.)
End of an Innings, Dennis Compton
(Oldbourne, London)
The Best of the Best, Charles Davis
Our Don Bradman, Philip Derriman
(ABC Books)
From Bradman to Boycott, Ted Dexter
(Queen Anne Press)
England Test Cricketers, Bill Frindall
(Willow Books)

BRADMAN REVISITED

Cricket (Batsmanship), C.B. Fry
(Eveleigh, Nash & Grayson Ltd.)
A Life Worth Living, C.B. Fry
(Pavilion Books)
Cricketers' School, Walter Hammond
(Stanley Paul & Co. Ltd.)
Batting From Memory, Jack Fingleton
(Collins, London)
Masters of Cricket, Jack Fingleton
My Life Story, Sir Jack Hobbs
Godfrey Evans, Christopher Sandford
Gary Sobers' Way of Cricket, Sir Garfield Sobers
& Patrick Smith *(The Five Mile Press)*
Cricket Up To Date, E.D.H. Sewell
The King of Games, Frank Woolley
Dennis Compton, Peter West
(Stanley Paul & Co. Ltd.)
The Silver Lining, Cyril Washbrook
(Sportsguide Publications Ltd.)

NEWSPAPERS AND PERIODICALS:

The Times
The Daily Telegraph
The Daily Mail
Observer Sport Monthly
The London Evening News
The Cricketer International
Wisden Cricket Monthly
Liverpool Daily Post
Liverpool Echo
The Sydney Morning Herald

BRADMAN REVISITED

Sydney Mail
The Australian
Herald Sun
The Hindu